FLY FISHING IN
CONNECTICUT

FLY FISHING IN CONNECTICUT

A Guide for Beginners

Kevin Murphy

Wesleyan University Press
Middletown, Connecticut

Wesleyan University Press
Middletown CT 06459
www.wesleyan.edu/wespress

5 4 3 2 1

Library of Congress Cataloging-in-Publication Data

Murphy, Kevin, 1949–
Fly fishing in Connecticut: a guide for beginners / Kevin Murphy. —
1st ed.
p. cm. — (Garnet Books)
Includes bibliographical references and index.
ISBN 978-0-8195-7283-7 (pbk. : alk. paper) —
ISBN 978-0-8195-7284-4 (ebook)
1. Fly fishing—Connecticut. I. Title.
SH477.M87   2012
799.12'409746—dc23
2011049406

Dedicated To
Patrick "Paddy" Keane
Nephew, Godson, Fly Fishing Partner.
Plays The Cards He's Dealt,
Always Upbeat,
Solid Company On Any Trout Stream.

Table of Contents

FLY FISHING IN CONNECTICUT

Introduction

Why are most fly fishing guides 400 pages? It just doesn't make sense. Considering that there is no substitute for experience, the guiding principle of this book is to provide the essential information needed for fly fishing. The rest you will pick up later—from your own experiences, from other anglers, fly shops, magazines, web sites, fly-casting clinics, fly-tying demonstrations, and other sources. Another important point—this book doesn't mention any of the expensive, top-of-the-line fishing gear. Instead, it steers readers to quality equipment that can be bought on a shoestring budget. The complete outfit for a fly fisherman or fisherwoman today could run $2,000 or more; this book shows you how to get started with just a few dollars.

Let's begin with a word about the sport of fly fishing and why Connecticut is the ideal place to embark on your journey. First, the dirty little secret: In order to catch native trout, an angler must travel by float plane to a stream north of Lac Saint-Jean, Quebec. Lac Saint-Jean, about a hundred miles north of Quebec city, marks the northernmost reach of the provincial government's stocking programs. However, it is not uncommon for serious anglers to spend thousands of dollars on seven-day fishing trips to northern Quebec—700 miles north of Hartford, Connecticut. But the average weekend angler...?

So what about the quality of fishing below Lac Saint-Jean? Surely there's plenty

> An Angler is a person who fishes using a fishing rod and a line. Dame Juliana Berners is a famous angler from the 15th century. She used a fly fishing rig.

of fish and pristine spots to be found in New England. Well, it depends entirely on the sophistication of a state's hatchery and stocking programs. Happily for Connecticut residents, the state's DEP Inland Fisheries Division enjoys an enviable reputation, raising about 800,000 catchable-sized trout annually and stocking almost 300 pristine rivers, streams, lakes, and ponds. Trout are Connecticut's most sought after game fish, generating two million fishing outings each year.

While fly fishing in Connecticut, you will enjoy some of the most beautiful scenery on earth—the flora and fauna of a king's private game preserve. You'll see bear, deer, beaver, opossum, skunks, rabbit, ducks, geese—and, yes my fellow angler, you'll see plenty of trout. Count on it.

All the while, the waters of your favorite stream will massage your body until you are as relaxed as a tourist in New Brunswick. While fly fishing, you'll be pampered and soothed for the nominal cost of a Connecticut fishing license.

To some extent, you will learn about ichthyology, entomology, hydrology, hydrography, meteorology, and biology. Don't be intimidated. Your education will be slow and effortless.

You'll have the great satisfaction of catching fish in a very ingenious manner. Fly fishing has been called the most elegant way to catch fish and that sums it up magnificently. Join your forebears—Winslow Homer, Clark Gable, Ernest Hemingway, Buffalo Bill, Annie Oakley, Zane Gray, Grover Cleveland, Teddy Roosevelt, Calvin Coolidge, Dwight Eisenhower, Ted Turner, Tom Brokaw, Meg Whitman, and thousands of other famous and not so famous Americans— and learn the delights of fly fishing. There's no better place to learn than on one of Connecticut's wild and scenic trout streams.

As with all sports and pastimes, fly fishing has its own peculiar vocabulary. You'll find help in the sidebars, and a full glossary at the end of the book.

Any reference to fly shops or equipment manufacturers is not meant as an endorsement. I scoured the fly-fishing world for the latest equipment and information—just as you must. If the name of a product, company, fly shop, fishing guide, or angler accommodation is mentioned, it is simply to get you started on your own search. I have received no compensation—financial or otherwise—from any equipment manufacturer, fishing outlet, guide service, lodge, hatchery, or anyone else connected with the sport of fly fishing.

A point of clarification: The state's fish and game department has operated under four titles over the past century and a half. From the Civil War until the 1920s, it was the State of Connecticut Fisheries Commission. During the Roaring Twenties, and for the next four decades, it was the State Board of Fish and Game. From 1972 to the mid-1990s, it operated as the Fisheries Division. Today it is called the Inland Fisheries Division. For simplicity's sake, the "fisheries commission" will be used until 1972, and "Inland Fisheries Division" from there on.

Lastly, I want to introduce a friend of mine, Sam Tippet. He'll share a few anecdotes and a wealth of tips on fly fishing. Sam knows all the tricks.

Sam Tippet Says-

Lefty Kreh, the great American fly fisherman, who served as a guide for the legendary Joe Brooks once said, "There's more B.S. in fly fishing than there is in a Kansas feedlot." I aim to demystify the sport by offering a few simple pointers from my forty years of fly fishing.

Chapter 1
Connecticut's Hatcheries & Stocking Program

On May 4, 1873, two Hartford men went fishing on the Farmington River in Granby and returned with 341 trout. Around this time, the *Hartford Courant* ran an article lamenting the fact that American shad in the Connecticut River were "rapidly diminishing in number... and size." Indeed, Barton Douglas, a longtime fisherman, operator of the Windsor canal, and owner of a ferry business, told the fisheries commission at the state legislature "shad fishing was nearly used up." Atlantic salmon in the rivers and streams of the state were virtually gone. The fisheries commission reported to the legislature that "the restoration of the salmon is the hardest task before the commission. At present they are nearly exterminated." In sum, by the late-1870s, Connecticut was almost fished out. Not surprisingly, the biggest culprits were over-fishing and market hunting. Other factors include the denuding of the forests—the natural canopy ensured cool water temperatures in the streams—and to a lesser extent, the construction of dams during America's great waterpower manufacturing boom of the nineteenth century.

> American shad, or *Alosa sapidissima*, meaning "most delicious," swim upstream from marine waters to spawn in the springtime.

Leading up to the complete decimation of the fish population in the state, the legislature had not been completely idle. In its 1860 spring session, the General Assembly announced a fisheries commission. A year later, Connecticut's first fish and game laws were passed. As regards trout, the statute read, "That any person... between the first day of September and the first day of January, in any year... catch... any speckled brook trout, or speckled river trout, or lake trout, shall forfeit for each trout the sum of one dollar...." However, there was no mention of fish size or creel limit.

In the absence of any fish and game wardens—and recognizing the fast-diminishing fish populations in the state's rivers and streams—a Poquonock father and son team of farmers, Fred and Henry Fenton, petitioned the legislature for a charter for a fish-hatching business in 1872. On Champion Brook, a small tributary of the Farmington River, the two Fentons raised Atlantic salmon and trout. The fish were fed ground sheep's liver, three times a day. This diet dulled the trout's vivid colors, and many of the trout lost their bright spots entirely. Fortunately, the condition remedied itself shortly after the fish were released into the wild.

> A creel is a basket used to carry fish. "Creel limit" means the number of fish you can take home in your basket.
>
>

> There are two types of Atlantic salmon, those that spend part of their lives in salt water and those that complete their life cycles in fresh water; but the two types were not recognized until about 1896.
>
>

In 1881, the Fenton Trout Breeding Company raised 600,000 Atlantic salmon and 275,000 brook trout, which were sold to the state. Soon thereafter, the Fentons managed three hatchery buildings with a breeding capacity of two million eggs behind their farmhouse. In 1882, rainbow trout were imported from California for streams that couldn't support brook trout because of higher water temperatures. (German brown trout eggs were shipped from Baron Lucius von Behr's private estate in the Black Forest to a newly completed hatchery at Cold Spring Harbor on Long Island in 1883, but brown trout did not show up in Connecticut waters until a decade later.)

The state was a bit gun-shy about starting a permanent fish-breeding business of its own though, as the fish commissioners noted, "it would cost too much to establish a state hatchery." But from the start, Connecticut's inland trout and Atlantic salmon efforts were a bargain. In 1882, a *Courant* reader complained of the cost of running the state's

Trout fry are baby trout. Fry, borrowed from the French word *frai*, literally means spawn.

fisheries. At that time, the cost of the hatchery purchases and the state's stocking program ran $690, while revenues from statewide taxation were $1.7 million. In answer to the subscriber's letter, an editor at the *Courant* performed some rudimentary math and concluded that the town of Windsor—where the subscriber lived—paid less than $1 a year toward the state's hatchery and stocking program.

By this time, Henry Fenton was the state's de facto fish-culture expert. Accordingly, the fish commissioners named him superintendent of the state's hatchery operations.

Beginning in 1880, as part of a new fish-stocking initiative, the state accepted applications for free trout fry from state farmers and sportsmen. One hundred and fifty applicants were each given 5,000 trout fry—in an eight-gallon can—at no charge. The state's only rule was that

Kettle Brook Hatchery, Windsor Locks

the fish could not be put into private waters; they had to be released into public rivers and streams. Five years later, thirty-five-year-old Henry Fenton was elected to the state legislature and became the conduit for all applications for free trout fry.

Finally, in the late 1880s, the fish commissioners—perhaps in a reassessment of Henry Fenton's fish-hatching monopoly—decided that the state should have its own trout breeding facilities and set up a temporary hatchery in the old Hathaway Mill on River Street in Poquonock. Fenton was placed in charge of this facility. Meanwhile, the fish commissioners badgered the General Assembly for the land and buildings to build a permanent structure.

In 1889, the legislature appointed Abbott C. Collins, an actuary with Connecticut Mutual Life Insurance Company and a fish commissioner, to the post of Game and Fish Warden of Hartford County for a period of two years. At the same session, the legislature set the catchable size of brook trout at six inches. They also noted, "It is unlawful to catch brook trout from July 1 to April 1, and then only by hook and line."

> Anglers often refer to brook trout, *Salvelinus fontinalis*, as brookies, hinting at a bit of playfulness—maybe because they are fun to catch, and plentiful.

Fish Commissioner Abbott Collins started the state's first permanent hatchery in 1897 on an eminently suitable 16-acre piece of land on Spring Street in Windsor Locks— a little over a mile west of the town's train depot. On a mile-long stretch of Kettle Brook, the state erected a crude, temporary hatching house with 15 tanks. That fall, hatchery employees released 35,000 brook and rainbow trout from 6-to 8.5-inches long, 20,000 lake trout from 5- to 6- inches long, and 60,000 Atlantic salmon from 2- to 3.5-inches long. A permanent hatchery building was finally completed in the fall of 1899. By December, the new facility set 1.5 million eggs a year, which produced 250,000 trout. (At this time, the state also had two shad hatcheries at Joshuatown in Lyme and at Peck's Pond on the Housatonic River below Shelton.)

Thirty-gallon cans of trout and Atlantic salmon fry were

*Rearing Ponds,
Kettle Brook Hatchery,
Windsor Locks*

shipped from the new hatchery in the fall of 1899 and the diversity of fish was remarkable—75,000 brookies, 40,000 lake trout, 6,000 rainbow trout, 15,000 steel head, 2,000 Loch Leven trout, 50,000 Atlantic salmon, and 15,000 of the land-locked variety.

The Windsor Locks hatchery on Kettle Brook was an enormous success thanks to its fabulous water supply. A number of underground springs supplied 300,000 gallons of water a day to the hatchery before it finally spilled out into Kettle Brook. The water was crystal clear and its temperature was a constant 53 degrees Fahrenheit year-round. Each November, the hatchery's 5,000 breeding trout delivered two million eggs, half of which would hatch out the following spring.

An important distinction between the fishing of the late nineteenth century and the early twentieth century, and that of a much later period, lay in the economic importance of trout, Atlantic salmon, and shad to the family table. The fish commissioners were

Suckers have no teeth and big lips, so they feed by vacuuming their food from riverbeds. They prefer clean, unpolluted waters and often swim with trout.

proud of the fact that these fish were often sold in local markets cheaper than "suckers" (freshwater fish of the Catostomidae family). Moreover, they wrote, "it cannot be many years before good edible fish will be produced (in Connecticut waters) in such abundance as to be within the means of the poorest." Beyond that, the fish commissioners were keenly aware of the symbiosis of good fishing and tourism, stating, "the state needs but plenty of fish and game to make it still more attractive to summer and fall visitors from other states."

In 1905, the legislature approved funds for a lobster hatchery at Noank. In the first two decades of the twentieth century, the state's hatcheries furnished brook, rainbow, and lake trout along with small-mouthed bass, yellow perch, American shad, and 125 million lobsters. A total of 130,585,830 fingerlings and fry were added to the natural compliment of fish and crustaceans.

> "Fingerling" means very young fish. The term most often refers to a baby trout or salmon that has reached the length of a man's finger.
>
>

Henry Fenton and a local worker, Gilbert Sterling, originally ran the Windsor Locks plant, but were replaced by William Tripp, who had been manager of the hatcheries at South Wareham, Massachusetts. Tripp was head of the Fisheries Division from 1898 to 1923. At that time, John Wheelock Titcomb—a man with thirty-four years experience in fish breeding in countries as far away as Argentina—became superintendent and William Tripp stayed on as the foreman of the facility at Windsor Locks.

The Kettle Brook Hatchery in Windsor Locks was a great success, but eventually deteriorated for the exact reason that it was such a world-beater from the start— the water supply. By 1923, the copious spring water had dwindled to a fraction of the 215 gallons a minute it furnished in 1897. Beyond this insuperable problem, fertilizer runoff from nearby tobacco fields despoiled the dwindling supply. Pollution regulation and source-to-sea cleanups were decades away. It was time for a new hatchery.

Loading a
trout-stocking
truck

Attempts to build hatcheries in Salisbury and Waterbury proved fruitless, and in the fall of 1923, the state bought land for a second facility in Burlington. The main hatchery was fabricated from the former dance pavilion at Electric Park in Rockville.

John Wheelock Titcomb's tenure was notable for the construction of the new state hatchery at Burlington and the leasing of trout streams throughout the state. While it was quite fashionable for farmers and sportsman to maintain their own trout streams and ponds, this behavior was circumvented in great measure by the leasing of streams for public use. "Gentleman George" McLean, governor of Connecticut from 1901 to 1903, had his own private fishing pond on his estate in Simsbury. Ineligible for state-bred trout, he paid $4 per thousand trout brought in from a hatchery on Cape Cod.

On the financial side, in the first ten months of 1924, there were 44,671 angling licenses sold in Connecticut. Residents—totaling 33,583—paid $1; non-residents—715 with land in the state—paid the same; another 4,312 non-residents paid $2. The $49,013 in licensing revenues completely paid for the state's hatcheries program.

Titcomb's successor, Dr. Russell Hunter of Wethersfield —whose tenure stretched from 1938 to 1953—summed up the role of head of the Fisheries Division succinctly in 1951 when he stated that his primary job was "enforcement." He also went on to say, "One of the biggest problems... is to rearrange nature to please fishermen... lakes and ponds are so equipped as to support practically a fixed weight of meat (fish) at all times. The ponds provide algae and plants for the plant-eating fish and enough plant-eating fish to sustain the fish-eating fish. Year after year, this underwater battle for survival goes on and the weight of fish in the pond stays about the same. The problem... is to rearrange all of this so that the fixed amount of fish will be in the right species, weights and limits to please the fishermen." During Dr. Hunter's time, only half of the trout needed were supplied by the hatcheries at Windsor Locks, Burlington, and Kensington. The rest were purchased from commercial breeders. By the early 1950s, enforcement officers spot-checking anglers' catches throughout the state had risen to thirty-five.

In order to meet the growing need for trout, small rearing stations were built in Farmington and Voluntown. Still, by 1970, the existing hatcheries could only meet half of the state's trout stocking needs. Another 30 percent came from commercial growers, and the U.S. Fish and Wildlife Service supplied the last 20 percent. Since the state was raising

I love to visit the hatcheries. Both hatcheries give free tours to the public seven days a week. Be sure to call ahead— Burlington Hatchery: 860-673-2340 or Quinebaug Valley Hatchery: 860-564-7542. The Quinebaug Valley facility has exhibits that are fun to tour. In central Connecticut, a trip to the aquarium at Cabela's in East Hartford is well worthwhile. Their trout are from Rowledge Pond Aquaculture of Sandy Hook, a private hatchery.

Sam Tippet Says-

trout for half the cost of those bought from commercial growers, it seemed like a particularly opportune time to erect another hatchery.

The Burlington Hatchery worked the western part of the state, and the Windsor Locks facility—older and smaller—stocked the northern reaches; so an enormous new trout-breeding plant in eastern Connecticut made sense. On 1,200 acres between the Quinebaug and Moosup rivers, the massive Quinebaug Valley Hatchery in Plainfield was completed in 1971. At the time—and even as late as the mid-1980s—it was the biggest fish hatchery east of the Mississippi River. That same year, the Kettle Brook Hatchery closed and the Town of Windsor Locks bought the land. Not long after, the Kensington Hatchery began raising Atlantic salmon as Connecticut's part of an inter-state/federal program to re-introduce Atlantic salmon back to the waters of the Northeast. Connecticut essentially

A boy bringing a trout to net

has only two trout hatcheries now—Burlington (15 miles west of Hartford) and Quinebaug Valley (38 miles east of Hartford) in Plainville.

If Connecticut is the gold standard in hatcheries and trout stocking, how do neighboring states fare? For many years, a New York visitor's fishing license permitted angling in many trout streams in the Adirondacks on a whirlwind expedition to the Empire State's northernmost reaches—the fabled Battenkill (on the New York side), the lovely and exciting West Branch of the Ausable, the North Branch of the Saranac, the Salmon (near Malone, where mobster Dutch Shultz once stood trial for bootlegging) and finally the Chateauguay River, in the apple country near the Canadian border. This fishing tour of the Adirondacks is not what it used to be. Sad to say, trout fishing is on the wane.

The same is true of other once-famous trout fishing areas of the Northeast. Anglers and state biologists suspect that acid rain, pesticide runoff, silt from stream bank erosion, and even geese have taken a toll on the streams and rivers. At present, states that are twice the size of Connecticut are stocking about half as many trout. The fisheries divisions of the New England states and New York are all trying to rebuild habitat and reinvigorate their trout fishing programs, but acid rain, deforestation, and budget cutbacks are impeding these efforts.

Stocking in Connecticut

Raising 800,000 trout a year would be of little value without tank trucks and the manpower to equitably release fish over the lakes, rivers, and streams of Connecticut. The Inland Fisheries Division has used basically the same model aerated tanker trucks to relocate trout since the late 1930s. It's a long process. Weather permitting, the first round begins in early March and lasts until the end of May. In 2009, for example, 55 to 60 percent of the full year's supply of trout was stocked by opening day—the third Saturday in April (6 a.m.). The remaining 231,000 trout are distributed in different ways on a variety of streams during the remainder of the season. In some places, there is only a single follow-up stocking, while in others, where the heaviest fishing pressures the fish population, trout are stocked until Labor Day.

All of the trout-stocking numbers can be found in the State of Connecticut Department of Environmental Protection's *Connecticut Fish Distribution Report*, but let's dissect a few number from the state's 2009 account just for the fun of it. Firstly, the number of trout stocked annually on the east and west sides of the Connecticut River are almost identical (West side–346,461; East side–356,287). Secondly, by watershed, trout are stocked as follows: Connecticut

> *The senior biologists at the Inland Fisheries Division say that in the areas where the creel limit is two fish, 90 percent of the stocked fish are gone in seven to ten days; in the places where the creel limit is five, 90 percent are gone in four days! Connecticut's trout fisher folks are short on patience. They follow the stocking trucks and leave when the fish aren't biting.*

Sam Tippet Says-

River watershed–211,245 (30% of the total); Thames watershed–195,056 (27.7% of the total); and Housatonic watershed–172,245 (24.5% of the total). Thirdly, the five towns (or town combinations) in Connecticut that received the most fish in 2009 were: Cornwall–18,000; Salisbury–14,316; Danbury-Milford–13,550; Eastford-Chaplin–12,824; and Thompson-Norwich–12,098. Lastly, if you add up all the trout stocked in the Housatonic River and the West Branch–Farmington River, it comes to about 22 percent of all the fish stocked in 2009 on the west side of the state.

Muddying the waters a bit, in eastern Connecticut, the levels of the Quinebaug, Salmon, and Natchaug Rivers get low in late

"Riparian" is derived from the Latin, *riparius* "of a natural riverbank," so a "riparian agreement" refers to a deal made regarding the fishing rights on the shores of a given waterway.

summer. The rivers whose water levels must be maintained by old riparian agreements—like the Farmington River (courtesy of the Metropolitan District Commission)—will by definition offer more consistent trout fishing throughout the season than rivers whose water levels are allowed to rise and fall with the seasons.

The streams of Connecticut's East and West sides vary in another way. In northwestern Connecticut, the trout waters flow easterly toward the Connecticut River. Thanks in large part to the Bolton Range—as high as 800 feet—the rivers and streams in the eastern part of the state flow toward Long Island Sound.

The best trout fishing in eastern Connecticut is spread out along miles of meandering streams that sometimes run almost the length of the state. The best-stocked bodies of water in eastern Connecticut are the Quinebaug River, Blackwell's Brook (and Kitts Brook) in Canterbury, and Five Mile River, running through Thompson, Putnam, and Killingly. The Little River, in Hampton and Canterbury, also benefits from considerable stocking. Owing to eastern Connecticut's wide-ranging diversity of rivers and streams, many of the finest fishing holes in that part of the state remain a secret to the very people who live there. (See Chapter 2 for some of Sam Tippet's favorite pools in eastern Connecticut.)

Here's a little known fact. The Inland Fisheries Division stocks the following urban ponds with about 10,000 trout annually — Beardsley Park Pond in Bridgeport, Keney Park Pond in Hartford, Lake Wintergreen in Hamden, Upper Fulton Park Pond in Waterbury, and Mohegan Park Pond in Norwich.

Sam Tippet Says-

Chapter 2
Connecticut's Trout Streams & Rivers

Since there is little fly fishing on lakes, ponds, bays, and sounds, a book on fly fishing in Connecticut must necessarily be about the state's many rivers and streams. Way back in 1880, Dr. William Hudson of Hartford claimed "Connecticut has some of the finest trout brooks in the world." Though he was obviously biased, an inventory of the state's many trout streams and rivers bolsters Dr. Hudson's stance.

For the beginner especially, knowledge of the state's new Trout Parks and its Trout Management Areas (TMAs) is imperative. In these areas, there are plenty of fish and

Every once in a while, someone asks me about saltwater fly fishing in Connecticut. It's a completely different sport than fly fishing for trout on streams and rivers. On Long Island Sound, an angler would use a #9 weight rod, reel and line with a leader that tapers down to 15 lbs. Striped bass can be taken on streamers (fished wet), and in the fall, Bonita and False Albacore. This type of fishing gained popularity in the late 1980s, but is on the wane now. Even when there is interest, saltwater fishing—of any kind—requires a different conversation than ours about trout fishing on inland streams.

Sam Tippet Says-

the beginner is far less likely to get skunked. Be sure to read the Connecticut Angler's Guide, Inland and Marine Fishing, available as a PDF or paperback booklet from the DEP and sporting-goods stores, where you'll find rules, regulations, tips, dates, photos, and a treasure chest of angling information.

"Skunked" comes from the Algonquin word squunck, and used as a verb it means, "to defeat." An angler who gets skunked tells us that the trout won the fishing competition and didn't get caught!

In the western part of the state, an angler can be assured of good trout fishing on the Housatonic River and the West Branch–Farmington. However, trout fishing in eastern Connecticut is more problematic. It is mainly a springtime activity, although excellent fall and winter fishing exists in a few streams.

Eastern Connecticut presents an ever-changing equation that bears study. In fact, the trout-fishing conditions east of the Connecticut River are so varied that whole books have been written about the rivers and streams crisscrossing this area. The Trout Parks and Trout Management Areas will get you started, but if you intend to spend your fishing career in the eastern part of the state, a book devoted solely to the trout streams of eastern Connecticut is highly recommended.

Sam Tippet Says-

In eastern Connecticut, I like the Salmon River from North Winchester to the Connecticut River—except in late summer when the water gets low. The Shetucket—for a few miles north of the Baltic Bridge—is good too. My last two favorite spots are the Natchaug in the Phoenixville–South Chaplin area and Merrick Brook near Scotland. There are some big browns in there!

The Quinebaug River runs from Massachusetts to Norwich, Connecticut and has the potential to be a great trout stream—perhaps even of the caliber of the Housatonic or the West Branch–Farmington in the western part of the state—but hydroelectric dams vitiate the potential of this

Comstock Bridge
over the Salmon River

river. The Quinebaug has a number of large and small public- and privately-owned hydroelectric facilities contributing to the regional power grid—Putnam Hydropower, Greeneville Dam (Norwich Utilities), Dayville Pond at Danielson (Summit Hydro Power), Tunnel hydroelectric dam (First Light Power), and the "L-shaped" Taft Tunnel Dam (Norwich Utilities) are the principal culprits. This is a river to watch though, as the Inland Fisheries Division would love to see it blossom into a first-class trout stream.

> *When the water gets low, trout hold in deep pools—low water means warm water, which trout can't tolerate. As you might imagine, areas with deep spots get overrun with anglers.*

Sam Tippet Says-

In addition to low flows and warm water, many of the best stretches of trout streams in the eastern part of Connecticut have limited access. Because so much of the land near streams and rivers is privately-owned, anglers aren't admitted. For example, the best part of the Salmon River is the lower four miles—below the Trout Management Area—which requires an angler to hike quite a distance. In the same vein, the Quinebaug could be a great trout stream, but it's hard to access in its lower reaches. The Inland Fisheries Division works continuously to gain access by way of easements, rights of entry, and other forms of admittance. (Usually, access to streams by land purchases is financially out of the question.)

On the other hand, some of the best stretches of the Natchaug and Shetucket have acceptable access for most of their runs. By and large though, the trout streams of eastern Connecticut are a trickier lot, made challenging by their uncertain flows as a result of dry weather and dams at Scotland, Occum, Greenville, Danielson, Jewett City, Mansfield Hollow, West Thompson, and Willimantic. A couple of these dams are hydroelectric facilities made functional by the disgorgement of large amounts of water during times of peak electricity demand. The operation of these hydroelectric dams makes water flows uncertain and wading sometimes exceedingly treacherous.

Some of the smaller streams of eastern Connecticut stay cool enough to support trout almost year round, but the larger streams heat up too much in the summer to offer much sport. Still, the peculiarities of the trout streams east of the Connecticut River won't be a concern for the novice who sticks to the Trout Parks and Trout Management Areas.

Trout Parks

In Connecticut's new Trout Park system, eleven "fishing holes" have been set aside for beginners, where the odds of catching trout are somewhere between an ironclad promise and a mathematical certainty. You can practice wading, casting, and learn to let your leader roll over nicely to deliver the fly to the exact spot desired. When using a dry fly, these protected bodies of water are also an excellent place for you to learn what a "drag-free" presentation looks like. That knowledge will come in handy later. The creel limit is two trout a day—of any size. The Trout Parks are located in easily accessible areas and are heavily stocked on a weekly basis to enhance the fishing experience for children and families, as well as those with limited mobility. There is also ample parking at the Trout Parks. Here are Connecticut's eleven trout parks, by town:

Western Connecticut

Kent .... Kent Falls State Park

Killingworth .. Chatfield Hollow Pond

Monroe .... Great Hollow Pond (Wolfe Park)

Oxford .... Southford Falls Trout Park

Simsbury .... Stratton Brook State Park

Wallingford.... Wharton Brook State Park

Watertown ..... Black Rock State Park's Branch Brook

Eastern Connecticut

Colchester ..... Day Pond

Eastford.......... Natchaug River Trout Park

Norwich......... Spaulding Pond

Vernon .... Valley Falls Pond

Trout Management Areas

After you've polished your casting skills and mastered the art of wading to the point where a trip to a serious trout stream would not be inherently dangerous, then and only then, would graduation to a Trout Management Area (TMA) be in order. The idea for Trout Management Areas in Connecticut was conceived a few decades ago. By conducting surveys from the late 1980s to the mid 1990s, the state firmed up a plan to stock the most desirable fish in these protected areas. The TMAs were instituted in 2001 and smaller creel limits and length requirements were adopted in order to ensure the viability of these unique areas.

Connecticut has fifteen Trout Management Areas: Naugatuck River, Bull's Bridge, Farmington River, Hammonasset River, Hockanum River, Housatonic River, Mianus River, Mill River, Moosup River, Pequabuck River, Salmon River, West Branch–Farmington River, William "Doc" Skerlick Saugatuck River, Willimantic River, and Yantic River.

These TMAs have various catch-and-release provisions, and generally have more fishing pressure than other areas. After you've fished the Trout Parks for a while, the TMAs are the perfect place for you to get some "on stream experience." With their higher catch rates, they keep boredom at bay while skills are honed. The TMAs have area-specific regulations such as "fly fishing only" and "catch-and-release only." (Go to the Connecticut DEP web site, found in the back of the book, for up-to-date information.)

Beyond the Trout Parks and the Trout Management Areas, there are hundreds of miles of rivers and streams in Connecticut for anglers to ply their trade. After practicing in the Trout Parks and TMAs, you'll acquire the skills to manage wilder areas and can branch out. At that point, Sam Tippet's favorite fishing holes—mentioned throughout this book—may be of use.

Sam Tippet Says-

There's generally good trout fishing above and below these TMAs too, although fishing season regulations apply. Catch-and-release TMAs can usually be fished all year round. Hearty folks fish them even in January, but when the water temperatures get below 45–50 degrees, trout get sluggish and don't eat much. I prefer the warm-weather fishing.

Chapter 3
Trout & Their Habits

Trout belong to the family *Salmonidae* whose members include Atlantic salmon, char, and whitefish. Members are commonly referred to as *salmonids*. The three most common trout—and the ones stocked in Connecticut—are rainbow, brown and brook trout. The rainbows spawn in the spring; the browns and brookies in the fall. Other fish that an angler will meet in the rivers and streams of the state include tiger trout (brown/brook hybrids that do not reproduce), and Atlantic salmon. However, this text is limited to the three trout most common in Connecticut's inland waters.

The brook trout is the only true native of the area, and is the most sought after of the three types of trout among long-time fly fishermen and fisherwomen. Thus, the expensive trips into northern Canada to catch native brookies or "squaretails." Brookies have long streamlined bodies and a rather large mouth that extends beyond the eye. They have a silvery white belly, sides of olive-green or blue-gray, and thoroughly unique worm-like markings along their backs and on their dorsal fin. Brook trout require cool, clear, stream-fed pools.

The rainbows are the most beautiful of the three species. Their body color is dark olive or blue-green on the back, blending into a silvery blue on the underside. Reddish-pink to light tan stripes and spots run down their sides, and an eerie sheen of mother-of-pearl helps to correctly identify this fish. Rainbows range in size from nine to eighteen inches in Connecticut waters. They are ravenous eaters and have been known to eat shiners—small silvery minnows—up to a third of their length.

Brown trout (German brown trout) have large black, and sometimes reddish-orange spots on the upper half of their torsos. A pale border of silvery brown borders their lower sections, and they often present a white belly. However, brown trout colors range quite a bit more widely than those of brookies and rainbows. Generally speaking, if you catch a trout and don't see worm-like markings on its upper surfaces or reddish-pink stripes down its sides, what you have is a brown trout.

Sam Tippet Says-

For my money, rainbows are the best fighters, perhaps because they are more acrobatic than browns or brookies. For every angler who agrees with me, there's another who likes browns and still another who prefers brookies. One man's brown is another man's brookie!

Trout have "lateral lines" down both sides of their bodies that allow them to sense barometric pressure, and alert them to approaching fish, anglers, and other possible threats. When a storm front comes in, barometric pressure falls, and these lateral lines tell the trout to start feeding. If you can arrange it, try to go fishing when the barometric pressure is dropping.

These same lateral lines alert the trout when you make a lot of noise walking and splashing in a stream, even when you are trying to be quiet. The speed of sound is more than four times faster in clear water than in air. Therefore, you might say trout are infinitely better equipped to sense you than the other way around. By working your way upstream as you fish, trout are less likely to intuit your approach.

Conversely, after a rainstorm—especially if the banks of the river or stream have been scrubbed a bit and the water is a little discolored—trout have a difficult time seeing insects and other food sources. At this time, an angler must use bucktails or streamers, and if these flies have a little shiny gold or silver on their bodies, so much the better.

Bucktails and streamers are types of fly fishing jigs that mimic baitfish. You'll learn more about those later. We don't know for sure how the term "jig" came about to describe the fake bait used to lure a fish, but notice how your fly does a little jig, or dance, when you cast it into the stream.

There are many different traveling and feeding patterns for brookies, browns, and rainbows. You can spend the rest of your life reading about these preferences or you can simply make a few mental notes as you begin to catch fish. What is the weather like? Is the water warm or cold? Is the water clear or discolored? Are you fishing in fast moving water, in a quiet pool, or somewhere between? What kind of fly are you using? In time—and without much effort—you'll build a database in your mind on the most intimate details of your catches.

Though it's only marginally important here, when trout "mate," they do so in an unusual way. The female lies on her side and creates a redd by digging sand and pebbles in the river bottom with her tail. She'll pick an area that is shallow and gravelly with a gentle flow of clear water. Then, she'll deposit her eggs into the little space she's cleared. Male

Patrick Keane landing a trout on the West Branch of the Farmington River

trout fight wildly for the right to fertilize the eggs. After the strongest of the males has won the battle and exercised his franchise, the female covers the fertilized eggs with sand and gravel, and swims away. This knowledge probably won't help you catch more fish, but it'll alert you to unusual trout behavior—and slightly different body coloring—during spawning season.

Besides swimming, trout do only four things—eat, void, sleep and mate. Fortunately for us, they spend most of their time eating. If you can learn to delicately put a fly of the right size, shape, and color in front of a trout, you'll catch fish all day long.

Sam Tippet Says-

As previously mentioned, trout spook easily. They are known for their alertness and awareness of their surroundings, so don't advertise your presence. Trout have a number of natural enemies—including anglers—so they are always on guard.

When hooked, spooked, or alarmed, trout burst for cover. This can range from the shade of an overhanging bank or tree branch to underwater rocks. After you hook one—especially the more powerful swimmers—like the large brood stock that the hatcheries throw in for their sheer excitement value—prepare for this burst because this is where the line can get snagged on rocks or a sunken log enabling the trout to break free.

Catching the Big One

Here are some pointers on what to do and what to avoid in your quest to catch the big one: If you're using a dry fly (more on the different types of jigs later) and you want to fool a trout into thinking it's the real thing, you must avoid

Tatiana Lvov fly fishing on the Farmington River

drag. The very second your fly begins to get dragged by the current, that cast has become worthless because the trout senses that your fly isn't a natural. In a big pool with slow-moving water, sometimes your fly can float the length of the pool without succumbing to drag. This is ideal. At all costs, you *must* avoid drag. In faster moving water, try making shorter casts and float the fly for a shorter distance. Another method you will see other anglers using as soon as you hit the stream is that of "mending your line." After you've cast, you simply use the tip of your rod to "flip" the midsection of your line upstream eight to ten feet. This buys precious time. As the current pushes your line downstream, it will take longer for your fly to get dragged.

Fish the big, placid pools—scattered within fast moving waters—where trout are using rocks, boulders, and sometimes logs as refuges. They can hide behind these obstructions for hours, expending very little energy. Trout tend to hold near the head of a pool where the cooler water

It sounds unlikely, but I got skunked my whole first season. Thirty-five years later, I taught my nephew and he caught a big rainbow on a dry fly the first time out!

Sam Tippet Says-

enters and there's more trout food coming their way. (We'll get more specific about trout food later in this chapter.) Often a river narrows and all the trout food is funneled toward one section of the river, dumping it heavily at the headwaters of a nice pool. This is why the top of a pool yields such good results and why the biggest fish take these choice-feeding spots.

Sometimes the tail end of a pool can deliver a nice surprise, but smart anglers go for the head of the pool first. Also, the headwaters, or upper section of a stream closest to its source, are generally better on low-flow, hot summer days, because the water is cooler.

Trout are opportunistic feeders, and when a certain group of insects are abundant, trout will focus on them almost exclusively. Trout often feed in a "feeding lane" in which trout literally line up to feed. When your dry fly is in this feeding lane, never try to retrieve it. Allow it to drift all

Patrick Keane shows off a nice catch

the way past the lane, then when it is directly downstream of you, give it a few gentle tugs, trying to get a trout to go for it as a wet fly—or perhaps a fly that is in the *spinner* stage of her life cycle. If nothing happens, take the line back into the air, and with as few false casts as possible, plop your fly back at its original mark.

Remember to be aware of the water temperature. Fly fishing for trout is most successful when the temperature of the water is between 53 and 63 degrees. Trout have to eat all year round, so there's plenty to catch in the colder months. Still, trout are sluggish in very cold weather and the odds are definitely not with you when the water temperature is 45 degrees or lower.

Trout don't sun themselves. At the high point of bright summer days, trout seek the shady spots in the river. Early in the morning and on toward dusk, they are more apt to venture into open waters to feed. The best time to fish the quiet, glassy meadow streams is when the skies are cloudy and there is a slight breeze to riffle the surface of the water. That way you can fish all day long, and if you're a late riser, you won't miss the fish.

Though many folks swear by it, I've never had much luck fishing before 8 a.m. and some of my friends claim to have had the best luck in the middle of the day. It might sound too good to be true, but you'll have the best luck when the conditions are the most enjoyable for the angler—around noon on cool days, and from suppertime until dark in the hot weather.

Sam Tippet Says-

When trout are feeding on the surface, they keep rising in the same spot. After you see a trout rise, try to mark the spot by aligning a rock or a tree on the opposite bank of the stream.

Just like everywhere else in this world of living things, the biggest, strongest trout command the best feeding areas. Identifying the best feeding areas is the heart and soul of fly fishing. Trout stream formations and water conditions add up to very good or very bad trout feeding areas.

White Water— Areas where the water is wild and moving very fast are practically worthless, because, as trout try to feed, the current sends them downriver and they are forced to expend precious energy to get back where they began. Ignore white water.

Boiling Water— These stretches are caused by quickly moving water hitting rocks and kicking up to the surface. When you see one of these sections, your first reaction may be to move on. This is a mistake. Trout are frequently on the move and a fly floating wildly down through these riffles will often prove irresistible. These can be surprisingly good areas to catch trout if it can be determined where trout food is funneling its way downriver. Look for places where quiet water meets the fast-moving, boiling water.

Riffled Water— This is an area where the stream narrows and relatively shallow water takes on the look of a washboard thanks to a rocky bottom. For some reason, this is an area that is often overlooked, but it can yield surprisingly good results.

Quiet Water— Quiet water usually means deep pools. Trout love these pools not only because they usually offer an abundance of food, but also because the water maintains a cooler temperature even in the dog days of summer. If the weather gets really hot and the sun is hitting the river hard, these same trout gravitate toward places where cool rivulets of water enter the stream or an underground spring filters in cooler water. Trout are always seeking food, but comfort is a consideration too.

Water Clarity— An angler must give consideration to the clearness of the water. Sparkling limpid water calls for longer leaders and thinner tippets. Fishing a shallow, clear stream on a hot summer day might call for a twelve-foot leader with a 3-foot section of 7X tippet attached. Most likely, your fly will have to be on a #20 hook or smaller. An angler who is new to fly fishing—and using a 7'6" or 8'0" rod—will have trouble handling a leader (with tippet) measuring more than ten feet. (For more about leaders, tippets, and rod sizes, see Chapter 4.)

Water Movement— Watch how water moves around a rock in the stream. The water behind the rock is still— sometimes referred to as tail water—while the water on both sides rushes past. The two places where the fast and still waters meet are called "seams." Typically, trout hold in the still water behind the rock and rise up to snap insects out of these seams.

A trout might travel sideways a few feet to grab a fly off the surface of the water, although the norm covers far less distance—often only a matter of inches. Sometimes, trout watch flies on the water for an interminable length of time while at other times they strike as soon as a bug hits the water. Almost always, trout feed in the exact spot over and over again. Oddly enough, as a trout feeds, the time between bites is very close to constant. After a trout has risen, count the number of seconds before it rises again. The idea is to synchronize your cast with the trout's next trip to the dinner table!

To get a day's worth of calories, trout would simply eat nice big shiners if they could. However, the opportunity isn't always there, so they are reduced to devouring hundreds of insects.

The three most important groups of insects to trout are mayflies, caddis flies, and stoneflies. Other insects that trout recognize as food are grasshoppers, leafhoppers, ants, gnats, crickets, beetles, spiders, damselflies, and mosquitoes. In other words, any type of insect found near trout streams. The "patterns" that anglers use are created to imitate these insects. This is especially important, as trout tend to concentrate on one type of insect at a time. If an angler isn't able to ferret out the proper imitation, frustration will be his or her fishing partner.

Mayflies

There are over 700 species of mayflies, but a Connecticut angler is only interested in a couple dozen of these fascinating insects. Their four-stage life cycle begins with tiny eggs, which are too small to be of any use to trout; it continues with the nymph stage, offering trout plenty of underwater meals; next is the dun stage—of supreme importance in dry-fly fishing—where the mayfly floats on the top of the water unfurling and drying its wings; and lastly mayflies morph into their spinner phase, where they are sexually mature and mate in mid-air—finally allowing the female to deposit her eggs on the water. These eggs eventually sink, and cling to rocks on the bottom of the stream where the cycle starts all over again. There are plenty of small variations, but this four-stage cycle applies to the vast majority of mayflies.

A "pattern" in fly-fishing lingo refers to dry flies and wet flies created to mimic live bait in action. You'll know when we are referring to the mimickers rather that their live counterparts by our use of capital letters. (A "Mosquito" is the name of the pattern; a "mosquito" is the insect it imitates.)

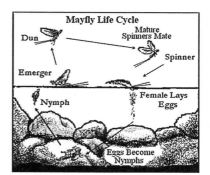

Caddis Flies

Adult caddis flies look a little like moths with hairy wings, and can be found in trout streams from April to November. Most species live in cases made of sand, shells, and debris held together with strands of silk secreted by the larva. Caddis flies usually produce only one generation a year and the adults rarely live longer than thirty days. These insects tend to be olive green or brown.

Nearly every trout stream in the United States has a caddis population. While caddis flies often appear in great numbers on Connecticut trout streams, they are challenging to imitate with a fly rod.

Caddis Fly

Stoneflies

Stoneflies are of much less importance than mayflies and caddis flies, although since they insist on cold, pure, well-oxygenated water—as do trout—they are worthy of our attention. Stoneflies tend to grow larger than mayflies and trout seem not to be put off by their larger profile. Adults display yellow to brown—not green—coloring with prominent dark patterns on the head and thorax. In the nymphal stage, they are usually found under rocks in trout streams. Stoneflies can be found in all U. S. trout streams.

Stone Fly |

A fly fisherman working the tail waters

The best trout fishing conditions occur when water temperatures favorable to insect activity coincide with water temperatures favorable to trout. Thus, trout will feed most when water temperatures are between 53 and 63 degrees. Mayflies will produce only one generation in a whole season and favor water temperature in the upper end of this range. When water reaches about 60 degrees, you can expect mayflies to emerge right on schedule, offering plenty of food for trout.

Hatches (emergences) may be delayed a bit by weather or water temperatures. Mayflies hatch annually in the same order with each species maintaining a certain slot relative to the others. Also, they hatch at roughly the same time each year. For example, in Connecticut the Quill Gordons are followed by the Hendricksons, and after the Red Quills come the March Browns. This holds true year after year. Understanding the chronology of mayfly hatches is essential to anglers.

Surface feeding is an activity that is brought about by the water presence of aquatic and/or terrestrial insects. Fly fishing for trout is not only a matter of what to look for, but once found, knowing what to do with that knowledge.

A blizzard of strange-appearing insects appears from nowhere and trout surface to feed wildly on them. This is the mayfly hatch. Most sport shops and organizations associated with trout fishing offer handy mayfly "hatch schedules" like the one on right for the different streams and rivers in their area. Look for them online by searching "Housatonic River Hatches" or "Quinebaug River Hatches," or perhaps the name of your favorite stream. For the hatch chart of a certain river or stream, check the Kynd Outdoors web site.

Farmington River Hatches

Insect	Size(s)	Mar	Apr	May	Jun	Jul	Aug	Sep	Oct
BWO	18								
Blue Quill	16,18								
Brown Stone	14								
Quill Gordon	12,14								
Hendrickson	10,12								
Red Quill	10,12								
March Brown	10,12								
Sulphur	14,16								
Green Drake	10 2XL								
Light Cahill	12-16								
Golden Drake	10,12								
Slate Drake	12,14								
Green Caddis	20,22								
Terrestrials	16-20								
Trico	22,24								
White Fly	12,14								
BWO	20-24								
Blue Dun	22-26								

These hatch guides are not foolproof, but endure as good representations of which mayflies should be on the river during a normal season. Notice particularly that a Blue-Winged Olive (BWO), a Green Caddis, and a few terrestrial patterns—beetles, ants, gnats, spiders, hoppers, and the like—can get a angler from Opening Day until late October. But just because the "hatch schedule" positions the terrestrials from mid-July through September doesn't mean that a trophy rainbow can't be caught in June on a Black Gnat or a Carpenter Ant. Moreover, there are forty-six different species of mosquitoes in Connecticut and a Mosquito dry fly is highly effective around dusk from May through September.

It may be impossible to talk you out of fishing on opening day, but hear me out. When fishing season commences in Connecticut, the streams are usually too high and the water too cold. Plus the waters are sometimes discolored with mud. Yet everyone in Connecticut who owns a fishing pole thinks about heading out that day. Sad to say, the number of fish in your creel is going to be inversely proportional to the number of anglers on the stream. Fish aside, opening day is a huge rush. I won't be the one to blame you for partaking, even if your luck would invariably be better a month later.

Sam Tippet Says-

Chapter 4
Getting Ready

Now the real excitement begins. What could be more fun than buying new sporting equipment? This chapter is a bit different though. Rather than tempt you with the finest—and most expensive—fly fishing equipment available, a special effort is made to feature equipment that won't break the bank.

Floatation Vest

Many novices will balk at wearing a life vest under their fishing vest, but it's a must. Angler expertise and experience have nothing to do with water safety, accidents happen. A Type III PFD (Personal Floatation Device) traditionally designates a PFD designed for inland conditions. This designation refers to watersport specific PFDs such as paddling PFDs, kayaking PFDs, canoeing PFDs and yes, fishing PFDs.

I'm quite fond of the Stearns Challenger Vest, a Type III vest at a bargain basement price. As a young buck, I often waded into dangerous waters. As a result, I took some nasty falls. Thankfully, I was wearing a floatation vest, as I still do most of the time. My nephew wears one too, and it has saved his bacon countless times.

Sam Tippet Says-

A Fishing Vest

You'll need a vest to carry your gear out onto the stream, but this is not the place to spend a lot of money. A poly/cotton blend lasts a long time. Vests that are all cotton start to look ratty after a couple of seasons. Be sure to buy a vest that is big enough to accommodate a floatation vest beneath it—along with a flannel shirt, jacket and sweater. With all the necessary layering, you'd be hard pressed to get a fishing vest that is too big! A good fishing vest has about sixteen pockets—inside, outside and even on the back—plus a couple of D-rings for attaching equipment.

Below is a list of items typically found in the vest of a veteran fly angler. While some items are essential, be assured that most anglers acquire these items over decades; so allow yourself plenty of time to do the same.

We are all part of the eco-system: insects; humans and other animals who live on land or in water; plants; fungi like mushrooms and bacteria; dirt and all the tiny microbes living in the earth; even air! So every choice we make has an effect on all other members of this living community.

"Putting down" a trout means to scare the wits out of it, so it darts for cover and forgets that it ever was hungry in the first place.

Trash Keep one pocket of your vest empty for incoming trash. Save all your used tippet and leader material, food wrappers and drink boxes. Take them home and dispose of them properly. It's our collective trout stream. Be a responsible steward of the ecosystem.

Tippet Material Every time you change flies, you lose a little tippet. A 30-inch tippet might be only 15-inches by lunchtime, so you'll have to have plenty of tippet material with you at all times. When the water is clear, you shouldn't let your tippet get shorter than 15 inches. Tippet material is inexpensive, so you won't want to waste time with a tippet that is too short. Rather than making convincing presentations, you'll just be putting down leader-wary trout.

Zingers, Nippers & Hemostats "Zingers" are little buttons with retracting lines that are pinned to the front of your fishing vest. Attached to each of these zingers are "nippers" for cutting off excess monofilament or tippet material, and "hemostats" for removing hooks from trout's mouths. You could buy a kit that included only a zinger, a nipper, and a set of hemostats. There is also a double zinger—with the nippers on one side and the hemostat on the other, plus a magnetic net release (to be attached on the back of your vest) thrown in.

Don't forget to check eBay. Here is an interesting find—a zinger, a nipper, and a set of forceps, packaged with a small ripple foam fly box—all for one price. Nice!

Sam Tippet Says-

Fly Boxes   Before 1860, flies were carried in leather "books." After that, they were toted in oblong tin boxes until around 1890, when Richard Wheatley introduced the first commercially produced tin fly box. Tin gave way to aluminum and, in 1908, Wheatley's compartmentalized fly box arrived. Wheatley's partitioned design has not been altered since. Today, plenty of manufacturers make cheaper versions of the classic Wheatley design.

Another choice for the beginner is the relatively new and exceptionally useful foam fly boxes made by Morell. These boxes allow an angler to hook his flies onto foam rows, thus preventing a minor catastrophe on a windy day. These nylon covered fly boxes even float.

There are plenty of environmentally-friendly models marketed too, but beginners should not get too carried away with fancy or expensive fly boxes. Any reasonable box—measuring about 4″ x 3″ x 1″—can be re-purposed to make a nice fly box, so long as caution is exercised when opening the lid on windy days! Look for fly-box contenders

I once met a guy who kept his flies in an old videocassette case that he fitted with a piece of his old yoga mat. He glued it in there with some strong, waterproof glue—and voila!— all his flies were lined up as neatly as trout in a fish market.

Sam Tippet Says-

at tag sales, secondhand stores, hardware stores, your kitchen cupboards, garage and basement.

Split Shot Split shot are tiny balls of lead or tin—slit almost in half—used to weight down your leader. You slip your line into the slit and then crimp it with pliers or your teeth. Packing a small amount of split shot is a good idea. (Take note: In some areas lead split shot is illegal, because it can cause lead poisoning to waterfowl. Be sure to check local fishing regulations before using it, or even better, stick to tin, like the environmentally-conscious line made by Water Gremlin).

Sometimes—and just for a short time—you may want to try a Muddler Minnow or a bucktail; and this can be accomplished by forcing your floating line to sink a little with a piece (or two) of split shot attached to your leader—either right up against the head of your fly or a couple of feet up the line. This method is often faster than changing spools and then switching back.

Mosquito Repellant Definitely get some good mosquito repellant. Mosquitoes seem to be worse in swampy areas and they are a particular curse in the twilight hours. At different times of the year, black flies and other pests may be a problem too. Unless you want your day spoiled, use a good, non-toxic bug repellent that will keep the bugs off you, but won't pollute the water.

Sun block Yes, keep some sun block in your fishing vest. The whole human race seems to underestimate the harmful effects of excess sun exposure. Let your catch be the ones to be cooked until crispy and brown, not you!

Under no circumstances would I encourage anyone to smoke. I can only tell you that I've always enjoyed a cigar while fly fishing. You don't need to inhale a cigar to enjoy it, and a cheap cigar—which smokes like a house on fire—keeps mosquitoes away.

Sam Tippet Says-

Water Bottle You can either invest in a fancy filtering system that allows you to drink from the stream, or you can fill up your canteen before you leave your house or fishing lodge. But, do remember to bring water. It would be embarrassing to dehydrate while standing in a river.

When I first started fly fishing, Giardia and Cryptosporidium were unknown. When thirsty, I drank from the stream. Times change. Bring along a water bottle filled from home. I never pay for store-bought water, what's the point? I'll just end up with more recyclables to deal with.

Sam Tippet Says-

Rain Poncho If you are the hearty type who wants to fish under all circumstances, you'll need a packable poncho tucked in the back of your fishing vest. On the other hand, if you are one who only wants to fish when the weather is pleasant, you should still pack a poncho, just in case.

First-Aid Kit Another just in case item you might consider keeping in a pocket is a small first-aid kit. You never know when you might need a bandaid or something.

Hat

At the very minimum, an angler should wear a baseball cap. The visor will cut down the glare from the sun and help keep floating flies in sight. However, in hot weather a ventilated hat with a nice wide brim all around is a better choice. If you've ever suffered sunburn on the tops of your ears, you'll be an easy sunhat proponent.

I wear the Redington Blackfoot River model fishing vest in tan. It has plenty of pockets and is made from a durable poly/cotton blend. I make it a point to dress in earth colors while on the river—browns, dark greens, grays and tans. The idea is to blend in with your surroundings.

Sam Tippet Says-

Polarized Sunglasses

Speaking of keeping floating flies in sight, polarized sunglasses help immensely. Instead of light scattering in all directions, reflected light usually travels in a more horizontally oriented direction. This creates an annoying light that we experience as glare. Polarized lenses contain a special filter that blocks this type of intense reflection, reducing glare. Let's face it, the really great anglers don't wear shades as a fashion statement!

Waders

You also need the proper kind of waders for the particular water and streambed conditions. Inexpensive rubberized canvas waders come with cleated soles. These are fine in sand and gravel, but come up short on slippery, rocky streambeds. Anglers used to glue felt to the soles of waders, but felt soles have been banned by some states—and Trout Unlimited. The interstitial nature of the material contributes to cross-stream contamination by Aquatic Invasive Species (AIS). In Connecticut, zebra mussels, Eurasian water milfoil, and particularly the nuisance diatomaceous alga, Didymosphenia geminata,or didymo—(rock snot)—now threaten to cross-contaminate Connecticut's beautiful inland trout waters.

> Trout Unlimited is a group of more than 140,000 volunteers organized with a common mission to "protect and restore North America's coldwater fisheries and their watersheds."

The environmental issues raised by felt soled waders limits those of us who use the rubberized canvas variety to the least dangerous sections of trout streams. For the beginner, this is actually a blessing. You should recognize the limits imposed by cleat-soled waders and plan your fishing accordingly. It makes infinite sense to start with a pair of inexpensive canvas/rubber waders until the love of fly fishing becomes an immutable fact of life. At that point, you can graduate to something more advanced.

Wading Staff

Old-timers like A. J. McClane and Lee Wulff have fished without wading staffs, but these "third legs" offer such a huge safety advantage to waders, they should be considered mandatory equipment nowadays. (Attach it with a three-foot piece of clothesline rope, so that it can float next to you when not in use.) Wading staffs probably reduce the odds of a fall by 50 percent, but even a much smaller percentage would make them worth their weight in gold. If you don't want to purchase a wading staff, then use a sturdy branch, or an old ski pole—either will work just fine!

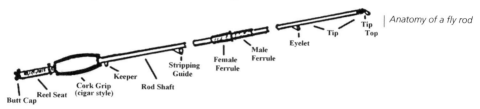

Anatomy of a fly rod

Tip
Tip Top
Eyelet
Male Ferrule
Female Ferrule
Stripping Guide
Keeper
Rod Shaft
Cork Grip (cigar style)
Reel Seat
Butt Cap

The Rod

Some long-time fly fishermen and fisherwomen are abandoning the graphite rods and going back to their old fiberglass models—rods that have roughly the same action as bamboo (Tonkin cane) rods—because they feel that the fiberglass rods load better. And, some anglers have even gone back to bamboo rods. To each his own.

Fly rods are described as slow, medium or fast depending on how stiff the rod. An important difference between spin rods and fly rods is that spin rods have pliable tips, while fly rods are designed to bend uniformly

> When you pull your line up off the water—and first get it flying through the air—we say the rod is "loading."

> "It is a poor craftsman who blames his tools." I'd rather see a beginner show up at the stream with a long, one-piece bamboo pole than to hold off until he can afford a new IM-6 graphite rod. My first rod was a 2-piece Cortland 8´0˝ 5/6-weight fiberglass model that I bought at a yard sale for a couple of bucks. I still use it on smaller streams.

Sam Tippet Says-

Speaking of fly rods, I was fishing
the small streams of the Taconic Range near
Williamstown, Massachusetts, back in the
1970s when I ran into a local fly fisherman. Reggie
Galvin held a bachelors degree in Ichthyology from the
University of Massachusetts, and he was the first person
to teach me about the lateral lines running down the sides
of trout. Reggie was also a gifted fly fisherman and a
consummate rod builder. He had a complete shop set up
in his mother's dining room and made custom fly rods
for a fraction of what old-line companies were charging.
I couldn't resist. I had Reggie make me a 6'-0" 4-piece
fiberglass backpacking rod that I could slip in a suitcase
if I needed to. His mother, Jeanette, made a gray cotton
sleeve with separate compartments to protect the four pieces
and Reggie slipped the whole thing in a rugged twenty-
inch tube. I still have the rod and use it on small streams,
but I get the biggest thrill out of the inscription on the
shaft near the cork grip, "Custom Built by
Reginald C. Galvin, 7/7/77."

Sam Tippet Says-

over their length. If a fly rod does not have this uniformity
of bend, it will never load and cast properly.

You can buy a good 8'0" to 8'6" IM-6 graphite rod at
almost any fly fishing center. Whatever model you end up
choosing, just be sure that the rod is clearly marked for a #5
or #6 weight line. For example, if you go with the Pflueger 8'0"
rod, the recommended line is a #5, and if you go with their
8'-6" model, it's a #6 line. There is a tendency toward slightly
heavier lines nowadays, say, #7 or #8, but you'll probably do
better with a #5 or #6 line. These are the old standbys.

*Reggie Galvin
and his 6'0"
backpacking
fly rod*

The Reel

There are plenty of fine reel manufacturers—Orvis, Cortland, L.L. Bean, Scientific Angler, Redington, Hardy, Pflueger—the list goes on and on. While almost any fly rod will do, a little more attention has to be paid to your choice of reel. This is because almost all anglers carry a single reel housing and two spools—one wound with a colored floating line and the other with a green sinking line. This way, if an angler wants to switch from dry flies to wet flies, he can simply swap spools in the middle of the stream—a much simpler operation than removing the whole reel from the rod and attaching a different one.

An inexpensive 3 1/8″ reel—like the Cortland CDM 5/6 #599673—with an extra "mid-arbor" spool—should work fine. The mid-arbor reel is slightly larger than the standard-arbor version, and increases the speed of line retrieval without the need for loading up the reel with backing—cheap extra line—before wrapping on your fly line.

The Cortland reel mentioned above is of cast aluminum, with a durable matte black finish, and smooth center disk drag. You can get an extra Cortland mid arbor spare spool (#5/#6) at almost any Online fly shop.

When putting a rig together, just make sure to match the weight of the fly line on everything. If the rod says 5/6 line, make sure the reel says the same. Then buy a #5 or #6 fly line.

Some reels are so fancy, I call them "fishing bling." I've always used the inexpensive reels made by great old-line companies. My first Cortland lasted twenty-five years.

Sam Tippet Says-

The Fly Line

There are hundreds of fly lines on the market. Someday, when you are the best fly fisherman or fisherwoman on the river, you might want a scientifically engineered line to match your rock star status. But today is not that day! Buy an inexpensive #5 or #6 double taper line. The Cortland 333 yellow double taper floating #6 fly line—DT6F—is a solid value. If you can find a less expensive floating line, so much the better. After you have used a double-taper line for a couple of years, you can take the line off the reel and switch ends. When you've put it back on the reel, it's the same as using a brand new line.

Use an arbor knot to attach your backing material (extra line) or your fly line to the arbor of your reel.

Arbor knot |

One last point. You'd be best with a floating double taper fly line that comes with loops already built into the ends. If for any reason your line doesn't have the loops, make your own. With a razor knife, trim the very end of the line so it trails off to nothing. Then bend the line back on itself to form the loop, glue it with permanent glue like Krazy Glue™ and whip it with dental floss. A little more glue on the floss and you're done. This will allow you to attach your leader to the fly line using a clinch knot.

Improved clinch knot |

To tie a simple clinch knot, skip the final pass-through. For most applications, like tying a fly on the tippet, a simple clinch knot works fine. The improved clinch knot comes in handy when, for example, floatant makes the tippet slick and extra holding power is needed.

Special Combination Units

One way to save a great deal of money is to purchase a "combination unit," usually composed of a fly rod, reel, floating line, a couple of leaders and even an assortment of flies with a fly box. Try sticking to the best names in fishing—Eagle Claw, Cortland, Pflueger, and Redington.

Often marketed to young beginners, combo kits are appropriate for any age angler. The Cortland 333+ Youth Fly Fishing Outfit (Model 603028), for example, is a lightweight and balanced fly-fishing outfit and includes a graphite fly rod; fly line; a large arbor fly reel; tapered leader; backing; and a fly box. This rig is a solid value.

Pflueger's 3-piece, 8'0" fiberglass fly rod with cork grip, mated with a Pflueger #1094 single action reel—the simplest, lightest and most popular type of fly reel— is one of the real bargains out there. It includes braided Dacron backing, a level (not-tapered) fly line, and a tapered leader. Pflueger even throws in some flies and a fly box. A double taper line might be better, but this is such a tiny deviation from perfection, it's hardly worth mentioning. Pflueger has been making fishing equipment since 1881. This kit is rugged enough for even the youngest angler.

Sam Tippet Says-

The Leader

Inevitably a beginner underestimates the importance of the leader (including the tippet). Among the different duties of the leader, it must transmit the power from the line to the leader and thence to the tippet and fly. Secondly, it has to provide an almost invisible link between the bulky fly line and the delicate fly. Lastly, it must allow a fly to drift—without drag—to give the appearance of a naturally drifting insect. Obviously we are asking a great deal of a small piece of tapered monofilament line.

Let's simplify this. You can make your own tapering leaders by tying together a number of pieces of different-sized monofilament or you can just buy tapered leaders. (About 90% of all leaders used today are the store-bought tapered variety anyway.) For now, don't try to tie your own leaders. You will accrue very little savings when a 7.5-foot tapered leader—that might last you the whole season—can be bought a couple of dollars.

Almost all leaders made for use in trout fishing have a butt end of 0X (attached to the fly line) and a business end (tied to the tippet) that can range from 3X to 7X. You should start with a 7.5-foot leader with about 2-feet of tippet attached.

As a newcomer to the sport, you are forced into a less than perfect situation. Preferably in clear water—like that in most of Connecticut's trout streams—you would do best with a 12-foot leader and two to three feet of tippet. However, as a newcomer, you would never be able to handle such a long leader. Thus, you must begin with something shorter. As your ability to cast proficiently increases, and the skill needed to get the leader and tippet to roll over correctly develops, a longer leader can be quickly substituted. When using a dry fly, it's not usually necessary to cast more than forty feet. Shorter casts give you more

I saw a 4-pack of knotless tapered 7.5 feet, 6x (0x to 6x) leader on eBay at a very inexpensive price. I've used "house brand" leaders offered by most fly shops too. Even better, check out some of the web sites who sell only environmentally friendly gear, like recycled boxes, biodegradable tippets, leaders and lines, lead free fishing sinkers, products made from recycled waders, etc. In the 7.5-foot and the 9-foot leaders, the 4x, 5x and 6x are the most popular. Just buy one of these 5x or 6x leaders, put 2 feet of 6x or 7x tippet on the end of it and you're in business!

Sam Tippet Says-

No leader is invisible, but try this. Take a 3˝ x 3˝ piece of bicycle inner tube and rough it up with a steel rasp. Then slide the folded patch back and forth on the leader. Be very gentle when working on the tippet. This will take the "memory" out of the leader, and the dark residue will reduce sun glint and visibility.

Sam Tippet Says-

control and a neater presentation, and it is far less likely that drag will ruin your efforts—at the very instant when you are preparing for that heart-pounding moment when a trout strikes.

When you get your fly sitting on the water properly, and when your leader, tippet and fly float nicely on the water, you've correctly executed the "roll over."

Leader Repair (and tying your own)

Sooner or later, a beginner is going to lose half his leader because of chafing, abrasions, a snag, an accident, or a dozen other problems encountered on a trout stream. Thus, a newcomer must have a working knowledge of hand-knotted leader construction before heading out. Incidentally, old timers claim that the roll over of a hand knotted leader is superior to that of the machine-tapered leaders. This is the type of esoteric point that anglers love to debate by a campfire late into the night.

A typical leader (and tippet) in the 9´6˝ variety would include the following components—from the butt end of the leader out to the fly. Begin with a 28˝ section of .021 monofilament, followed by a 14˝ piece of .019 monofilament. Then add a 12˝ of .017 monofilament, a 10˝ section of .015 and a 6˝ piece of .011. Cap this off with 6˝ of 2X tippet material, then 6˝ of 4X tippet material. Lastly add 20˝ of 6X tippet material. This is an excellent knotted leader for a beginner, the sections held together with blood knots (shown below). Naturally, when a beginner loses half his leader, he must improvise with the different-sized tippet

Blood knot

West Cornwall
Bridge over the
Housatonic River

material in his vest and a little knowledge of hand-knotted leaders. Remember: Leader and tippets are always getting thinner and lighter as they work their way toward the fly.

Another leader knot, which has built up a respectable following in recent years, is the double surgeon's knot. (Still other anglers prefer the triple surgeon's knot because they insist that the double cants to the side whereas the triple lays nice and straight.) It is claimed that the double surgeon's knot is stronger than the blood knot and easier to tie. The first claim is debatable; the second is not.

Double surgeon's knot |

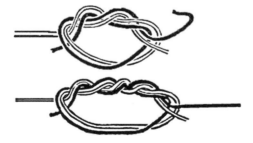

Triple surgeon's knot |

A final thought on leader construction. Most hand-tied leaders are based on the "60/20/20" formula. About 60% is composed of fairly large diameter material—like .021

monofilament; the middle 20% is made up of short pieces which rapidly decrease in diameter—perhaps .019 to .013; the final 20% is one or two pieces of fine diameter tippet material—maybe 5X and 6X. A leader employing this formula will roll over nicely.

The Net

The classic trout net is an oak-framed, teardrop beauty with green-stringed mesh. There is no rhyme or reason to this configuration—and there are plenty of other types of nets on the market. For example, there is even a net specifically designed for the catch-and-release throng, although many old timers eschew this model. Sometimes the old standbys are best. The one modern day improvement on the trout net that is worth its weight in gold is the stainless steel spring-leaded retractor. This metal devise—about the same size and shape of a pocket watch—clips on to the back of the fishing vest (near the neck), and allows the angler to reach back and pull out the net at just the right moment to land a fish. Otherwise, the retractor keeps the net out of sight and mind.

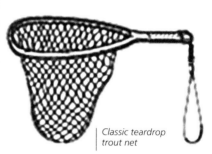

Classic teardrop trout net

The Creel

A creel is a canvas bag or wicker basket—with a shoulder strap—used to transport your catch. This seemingly incidental item separates the real anglers from the wannabes. The overwhelming majority of longtime anglers have no use for creels because they are part of the noble catch-and-release fraternity. Somewhere along the way they realized that when the fish are gone, so is the sport of fly fishing. In short, they leave the mindset of the meat catcher behind in favor of the enlightened thinking of true sportsmen. Don't worry, these folks won't laugh at your creel because they started the same way. They caught 'em, they bragged about 'em, they cooked 'em and they ate 'em. Now they've moved on. If you insist on a creel, get one of the cheap models secure in the knowledge that inevitably you too will one day enter the catch-and-release fraternity and forever after show up on trout streams "creel-less."

When using a creel, it's a good idea to mindfully cut some young fern fronds to line the bottom of your creel before you start fishing. While not absolutely necessary, the ferns will protect your catch. Never over pick, choose a few fronds from well-established fern beds, and be careful not to kill the whole plant.

Chapter 5
Hitting the Stream

Now that you've gathered together all of the necessary equipment, the next step is to actually start fly fishing. Ahhh, things get serious quickly. Hopefully with some good advise, you can make the transition from the sporting good store to the trout stream without winding up in the hospital with a fractured skull. Lurking just beneath the surface of every beautiful trout stream are hidden dangers that require your complete attention.

When putting the pieces of your rod together, be sure to line up the eyelets as best you can and twist gently as the pieces seat themselves. When taking the pieces apart, lay the rod against the back of your knees—horizontal to the ground. Then grab the pieces with your hands up against the outsides of your knees. Spread your knees gently and listen for the "pop." Never touch the ferrule joints when putting a rod together or taking it apart, because you might damage or loosen them.

Attaching the reel is simple, but threading the fly line can be frustrating unless you know one little trick. Don't thread your line through the eyelets of your fly rod by using the end of the tippet—this isn't like threading a needle. Instead, about six feet back from the end of the colored fly line, double the material over, and thread the line by pushing this loop through the eyelets. If you should let go of the line for any reason, it will be hard

Ferrule joints are the metal-banded areas where you can pull your sectioned rod apart for compact storage.

for the line to slip back through all of the eyelets. In short, you won't have to start all over again.

Threading a fly rod |

Another thing to take note of is the condition of the stream to determine what kind of fly to tie on first. If there's a Hendrickson mayfly hatch coming off the water, you can start with a Dark or Light Hendrickson dry fly. If there's nothing coming off the water, you may want to begin with an old standby like a Blue-Winged Olive, or perhaps a terrestrial like a Black Gnat or a Mosquito. After you have tied on the fly in question, dress your leader, tippet, and fly with the appropriate bicycle inner tube material and fly floatant (as discussed in Chapter 7). Then hook the fly on the keeper—the little ring just above the cork grip on your rod—and reel in the excess line. If you can keep some pressure on your leader and tippet until you are ready to start fishing, this too will help straighten them.

In real estate, it's "location, location, location." In fly fishing, it's "presentation, presentation, presentation." In dry-fly fishing particularly (see Chapter 6), presentation means entering a trout stream stealthily and unnoticed by your quarry. It means casting without disturbing the water, and of course it means landing the exact right fly—gently and quietly—upstream of where a trout is feeding. The fly will float—drag-free—over the spot where the trout is feeding on the surface and, hopefully, attract a strike. It does no good to have your fly float over the spot where a fish is feeding only five seconds after he has taken his latest morsel of food. Time your cast so that the trout has had time to enjoy his last snack and will be free to go after your offering.

With wet flies all the same holds true, except that you cast across the stream and let the fly float slowly to a point straight downstream. Ever so slowly, you bring the line in by layering 3-inch sections of line atop one another in your palm using "the hand flop" method of retrieval. (This maneuver is explained in the chapter on wet-fly fishing.)

Trout Handling

Trout have very small scales and also a protective film on their bodies. Therefore, whenever you handle a trout—to remove a hook, for example—be sure to first wet the hand that will do the gripping. By wetting your hand, you will avoid any damage to the trout's scales and their all-important natural protective coating. Every once in a while, you may catch a fish with an eerie white finger-shaped fungus on its skin. This is the result of inattention or ignorance and can be avoided with a modicum of care.

Sam Tippet Says-

Trout only do 10 percent of their feeding on the surface. This makes dry-fly fishing a real test of skill. There's nothing more exciting than casting a dry fly to a precise spot on a stream and then watching a good-sized trout snap it up. On the other hand, if you prefer to fish blindly while waiting for an almost imperceptible nibble on your wet fly at the bottom of the stream, I can't fault you—but we wouldn't make good fishing partners.

Streamology

Though not actually a word, at least not in Webster's book, streamology could be defined the same as hydrography— the study of flow of streams—with one very important addition. It is a study of the flow of streams—*to figure out where the trout are!* Of course, no one needs a fancy word to realize that the first task upon arrival at a trout stream is to survey the situation. Look for the pools, the rocks, the trees that have fallen into the stream, beaver dams or anything else that looks like a good place for trout to hole up. Take note of the time of day and the position of the sun. Remember that trout like cool water. Only after you have studied the whole area and mapped out a descent plan of attack, should you enter the stream—QUIETLY. Trout don't have ears, but remember, their lateral lines alert them to even the slightest vibrations and noises underwater. If one stone touches another—thanks to your clumsy wading—the trout will sense it.

Anglers love to rhapsodize about sixteen distinct splashes trout make when they rise. Supposedly, these splashes tell you a heap about the trout in question. Hogwash! In my favorite pools—where most trout are all between ten and twelve inches long—there are as many different kinds of splashes as there are minutes in the day. The only thing I'm sure about is that playful five-inch fingerlings make a racket when they break the water, while bigger trout nab flies from the surface with surgical precision.

Sam Tippet Says-

Casting

Casting is one of the reasons why this book isn't 400 pages. There've been million of words written about fly casting, but there is no substitute for experience. The main thing worth remembering is that in fly fishing you are using the weight of the line to propel the fly, while in other forms of fishing you are using the bait (together with assorted weights) to provide the carrying power. What truly matters in fly-casting is the experience you rack up with rod in hand.

Because I tend to cast with gusto, I have to be careful when using a 7x tippet. I have to slow my cast down so that the fly doesn't break off. The line and leader must be flat out on the back cast before beginning the forward cast. Otherwise, the tippet snaps like a bullwhip and breaks under the stress.

Sam Tippet Says-

There are in effect only two methods of casting a fly line—the traditional cast and the roll cast. Let's begin with the traditional cast.

The first lesson in fly-casting: Don't start on a trout stream. Start in your own back yard. After you have your rod and reel set up—perhaps with a 7'6" tapered leader and a 2' tippet—tie a small piece of white yarn to the end of the tippet, and start practicing. At first, just try to get the yarn floating through the air—back and forth, back and forth—without touching the ground. Use your forearm, not your wrist. Notice how you must pause a second after your back cast to make sure the line has time to completely lay out, or extend in a flat straight line in the air. Notice also how much more effective your casting is when you keep your casting elbow on an even plane with the ground, sort of like casting with your elbow on a shelf. And notice how little body motion is required.

The tip of your rod should travel between 9 o'clock and 1 o'clock, although Norman Maclean—in his autobiographical novella *A River Runs Through It*—remembers being taught that the movement should be between 10 o'clock and 2 o'clock. Just as in any other sport, there are as many different styles as there are players in the game. Fly-casting styles can be poetry in motion or butt ugly, but don't worry what you look like. Just get out there and the refinements will come with time.

After you have completed a multitude of false casts, see if you can land the yarn twenty feet to the right of that old apple tree stump. Oops. Did the whole leader collapse into a ball in the same spot? Try it again with the forward motion of the tip of your rod stopping at 10 o'clock. Better? Ultimately, trial and error will be your best teacher. Keep practicing.

Words of advice that could save you a ton of needless worry: There is a universal fixation among fly fishermen—they all want longer casts. Baseball Hall of Famer Ted Williams once had a fishing camp on the Miramichi River in New Brunswick, Canada, and was famous for adding twenty feet to the casts of visiting friends. Using salmon fishing gear, Williams' casts were said to average between eighty-five and ninety-five feet! Notwithstanding the persistence of this little casting obsession, the smartest anglers recognize that fly fishing, like baseball, is a much more complex sport than it appears. Trout can be caught all day long by folks who can't cast more than forty feet. The right fly on a near-invisible leader—coupled with superb presentation—will carry the day every time.

In the end, the difference between the true superstars of fly-casting and everyone else comes down to only two items—balanced equipment and practice. If you have the right rod and reel for the weight of line you're using, half the battle is already won. The second half is tougher, of course, because it takes many years of practice to rise to the level of a Lee Wulff, A. J. McClane, or Lefty Kreh. However, the wise newcomer will accept this as a challenge. To quote the famous angler Ralph Waldo Emerson, "When Duty whispers low, Thou must, The youth replies, I can!"

The second method of casting a fly line is the rarely used, but handy, roll cast. When trees, foliage, cliffs, or other obstructions are behind you limiting your ability to use a traditional cast, you'll be glad you spent just a few minutes learning to roll cast. This method is simplicity

I love to watch Lefty Kreh giving a fly-casting lesson on YouTube. The reason he is such a good teacher is because he can take the complicated and make it simple. He is so comfortable with a fly rod in his hand that he talks endlessly about technique while his line floats gently through the air. Oddly enough, Lefty casts with his right hand!

Sam Tippet Says-

itself. With your line laying straight out on the water, slowly lift the tip of your rod until it is pointed just behind your head. (The rod and loose line should form a capital D.) Then snap the tip of the rod forward and down toward the water, sending the fly line in a rolling loop across the water. The roll cast takes some getting used to—at first you run the risk of annoying the trout—but once you get the hang of it, this maneuver can be a godsend.

In the film version of *A River Runs Through It*, professional fly-casters were hired to create some truly memorable roll casts for moviegoers. Done expertly, a roll cast resembles the pinwheel in a Fourth of July fireworks display, but with water spitting off the fly line instead of sparks. Breathtaking!

With a little practice, you too can be a movie star. Picture this: A trout is rising to nab mayflies, caddis flies, or other winged insects. It's almost a dare. The trout is saying, "Here I am. I'm feeding. Let's see what you've got!" Moving stealthily, you cast your floating imitation so that it drifts naturally over the exact spot where the fish is feeding. In an instant, you see your fly disappear into the center of a small splash. With your fly rod poised out to the side—

Jason Borger, John Dietsch and Jerry Siem were hired as fly-casting and fishing doubles in Robert Redford's film version of Maclean's *A River Runs Through It.*

and the tip near the water—you give a small tug to set the hook, using the surface tension of the water to transmit the pull all the way to the fly. Immediately, you straighten the fly rod to a vertical position—where it acts as a shock absorber—so that your 6X tippet won't be snapped while the fish swims back and forth displaying an extraordinary amount of fight. You play the fish a bit, allowing it to scrub off some energy while it swims back and forth wildly. Then with your left hand, you slowly strip the line between your right index finger and the cork grip of your rod until the trout is "brought to net." Naturally, if a trout exerts more fight than expected, a little line must be let out so that the trout won't "break off." (An important difference between hook-and-line and fly fishing is that the reel is not used to land a trout.)

Before you get to be the angler in the movie, though, you must develop a healthy respect for the leader and tippet. When you are bringing in a fish, watch the tip of your rod to make sure that you never pull in so much line that the leader winds up in the eyelets of your fly pole, lest it break off. Without putting too fine a point on it, tippets are the weak spot in the whole system. Trout are never going to break your fly, but even a small trout can break your tippet by exerting just the right amount of fight at precisely the wrong moment.

Wading

It's a time-honored axiom of fly fishing that beginners wade where they should be fishing and fish where they should be wading. For example, an experienced angler knows that fish hold in the tail waters behind rocks. Naturally, the novice thinks fishing from these nice quiet spots would be ideal. Little thought is given to the trophy-sized rainbow trout that is holing up in that area. In the beginning, you should seek out places on the stream where the water is no higher than your knees, yet still within casting distance of the pools where the trout are holding.

The most important thing to keep in mind is that wading in trout streams can be exceedingly treacherous. So said, it's best to fish with a friend.

If a beginner is in fast-moving, waist-high water, the conditions are definitely there for a catastrophic—perhaps even fatal—accident. When a fly fisherman or fisherwoman takes a fall under these conditions, the rocks in the river, big and small, are not particularly friendly. One nasty head-butt on one of these rocks can cause serious injury, so beware.

Fishing a quiet spot
in hip boots

Streams are laden with marbleized rocks, algae-covered tree parts, sudden deep spots, and a host of other nasty surprises.

Owing to these dangers, the adage "an ounce of prevention is worth a pound of cure" has never been truer than in fly fishing. You should always wear a flotation vest underneath your fishing vest when doing any wading at all. This includes wading in the state's Trout Parks, which are calm and shallow. To prevent hypothermia, wear long underwear and jeans under your waders. On a July day, fifty-five degree water doesn't seem cold when you first get in, but you'll have an entirely different opinion after a couple of hours of wading.

Like in any sport, it pays to be in shape. In a perfect world, all fly fishermen and fisherwomen would be tall, narrow-hipped, broad-shouldered athletes, with more than the average amount of daring. While no angler is immune from the dangers of rolling rocks, slick surfaces, and the dozens of other hazards found in trout streams, a physically fit angler has a tremendous advantage over one who is out of shape. Nevertheless, respect and knowledge of nature and waterway ecosystems will help anglers at every stage of development.

Common sense is particularly important when wading across a trout stream. In places where the water is fast moving, try to keep your body turned sideways so the current has the smallest effect on you as possible. Essentially, you don't want to give the rushing water a big target.

Unfortunately, even the most cautious anglers take spills. It's unavoidable. However, a little knowledge can keep an embarrassing slip from turning into a catastrophe. To begin, always make sure the drawstring at the top of your waders is tied tightly, so that water has a difficult time getting in. If your waders have belt loops, be sure to use a belt. In the event of a fall, your knees will come up and the belt will tighten around your hips, thus limiting the amount of water that gets in. If you can get your feet under you, get up. But if you can't, no need to panic. Just lie on your back with your arms out and your feet pointed downstream. With any luck at all, you'll be able to get back up soon enough.

One last point. If you're having trouble balancing, lowering yourself deeper into slow-moving, thigh-high water will actually improve your balance and help you better negotiate an area that is giving you footing problems. And if you fall into the water, and no matter how hard you try, you just can't get up, don't be afraid to shout for help!

Waders inevitably spring leaks. Well before you head out in them, go to a darkened room and lower a drop light into your waders, one leg at a time. After you find the hole, mark the spot and then use a patching adhesive like GOOP™ to coat the entire area of the leak. Follow the directions for drying time, and you'll be watertight.

Sam Tippet Says-

Chapter 6
Fishing Conservation & Etiquette

Conservation begins with your treatment of the lands associated with Connecticut's fabulous trout streams. Try hard to leave the flora and fauna exactly as they were when you arrived. True, in the course of an average fishing season, you will find debris left by less-enlightened folk, otherwise known as litterbugs. If possible, pick up their trash and dispose of it responsibly with your own trash and recyclables. You may also find the carcasses of many different kinds of fish, birds, snakes and animals. Leave these alone and simply allow Mother Nature to do her work.

Barbless hooks are the way to go. They work just as well as the barbed variety, but spare the trout nasty damage in the mouth-and-throat areas that reduces their chance for survival when released.

Fishways. These "fish ladders" at dams are important components of enhancing Connecticut's protected watershed species. Fishways restore the passages between freshwater habitat and the ocean for migratory fish like Atlantic salmon, American shad, sea-run brown trout, and a number of other migratory fish. There are over fifty fishways in Connecticut. Anglers are prohibited from fishing in the areas immediately downstream or upstream of a fishway— generally for a distance of 250 feet. At some fishways, this distance may vary, but you'll find these variances posted. To learn more about fishways, read the state's Angler's Guide.

Protecting species and habitat. Don't catch trout in one body of water and then try to introduce them to another. The possibility of improving a river or stream is zero and the chances for introducing infection or invasive aquatic species across different bodies of water is enormous. The trout streams of Connecticut are magnificent, so there's no reason whatsoever for amateurish efforts to improve on them.

Protecting Atlantic salmon. Since the 1960s, the Inland Fisheries Division has been committed to a regional cooperative effort to restore runs of Atlantic salmon to the Connecticut River. Salmon runs are currently being developed on three tributaries of the Connecticut River— Farmington, Salmon, and Eightmile Rivers. Some Atlantic salmon are released into the Shetucket and Naugatuck Rivers for sport fishing. However, in most areas, Atlantic salmon may not be taken. Salmon can be confused with brown trout because the colorings of the two are similar. However there are differences, which should be noted. In order of identification ease, they are as follows: (1) Atlantic salmon have forked tails while brown trout have square tails; (2) Just ahead of the tail is the caudal peduncle. On salmon, this is narrow and tapered, while on a brown trout, it is thick and stocky; (3) The adipose fin on a salmon is gray to olive, but never orange. On the brown trout, it may be spotted with red or orange; (4) The mouth of an Atlantic salmon extends to the back of the eye, while it extends well past

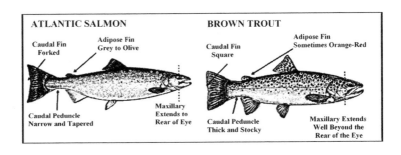

the eye on a brown trout. If you hook an Atlantic salmon, release it carefully back into the river the same way you would release a trout. Any doubts—release it!

Catch and release methodology. Since you will undoubtedly graduate to the noble catch-and-release class at some point, knowing the proper way to deal with your catch is mandatory right from the get go. After you have hooked a trout, keep in mind that you must not allow the fish to become completely exhausted. In playing a fish, you walk a fine line. If you try to horse him in too quickly, there's a strong chance he will break off. Obviously, this has a lot to do with the diameter of your tippet. Conversely, if you allow the trout to run to exhaustion, survival will be difficult after release.

> How do you "horse" a fish? Hopefully, you won't; but "horse" means to be aggressive in your retrieval.

After you have brought a trout to net, wet your hands before removing the hook. Usually a wet hand, cradled under the belly of the fish, is quite sufficient. Alternatively, slide your hand forward so that your grip is closer to the jaw. Use your forceps to back the hook out carefully. If the trout has completely swallowed the hook, it is better to cut the tippet off as close to the eye of the hook as possible and allow the deeply-buried hook to remain where it is. Trout hooks dissolve in a relatively short period of time.

Keep your catch in the water for as much of this release period as possible. Finally, with one hand under the belly and the other just ahead of the tail, gently slide the trout back and forth in the stream to circulate water across its gills. Don't let the fish go until it has regained enough energy to maneuver under its own power—and survival seems assured.

Any discussion about hitting the streams for the first time would be incomplete without a word about fishing etiquette. This is mostly a matter of common sense, which "is not so common," as Mark Twain once quipped. That said, let's list a few essential rules of conduct:

Give other anglers their space. Since trout spook so easily, don't think you can just start fishing twenty-five feet from another angler without any problem. Look for a nice run or riffle of your own. You can always double back and fish that pool later.

If you must pass behind another angler, try to do so on shore. If bushes, rocks, or other obstacles prevent this, then pass by as close to the stream bank as you can—and as quietly as possible!

First come-first served. The streams may have many different owners—including state taxpayers like you—but the first one to arrive at a given spot on the river has earned the right to fish there. So find another spot.

Don't spook another guy's fish. This shouldn't need a whole lot of explanation, but there are times where we all become absent-minded. Don't ever throw rocks, sticks, or other materials into trout streams. Trout spook easily, so take the necessary steps to respect another angler's environs.

Respect the law. Be sure to read the *Angler's Guide* published each year by Connecticut DEP's Inland Fisheries Division, paying particular attention to state laws, rules, and regulations. Creel limits differ and are set to ensure the viability of the sport. Trust me—no one wants you fishing in state waters if you can't obey some simple fishing laws.

Buy a license. Taken together, Connecticut's hatchery and stocking program is one of the few state services that makes money each year. However, that would change quickly if

Listen to the old-timers!
And, if an angler ever gives you a fly from his case, pull out your fly box and let him pick one of yours.

Sam Tippet Says-

everyone decided not to buy a license. Do your part to keep the program healthy by purchasing a license at your local Town Hall or sport shop annually.

Remember, private-property owners own the land to the middle of the stream that abuts their parcel. If you are wading, you need the owner's permission to be on the land. If you are floating in a canoe, kayak or tube, you do not need permission as long as you do not come in contact with the ground at any point. Get into the habit of seeking permission whenever you must traverse forests or meadowlands to get to a stream. If the land is not posted, cross discretely and without disturbing anything. If it's posted, obey the signs. Lastly—particularly in eastern Connecticut where so many of the smaller trout streams run through private property—recognize that you may happen onto private property as you wade upstream. Pay attention!

Chapter 7
Trout Food

Dry Flies

It is an enduring puzzle of fly fishing. Trout only take 10 percent of their nutritional needs from the surface of the water, yet the vast majority of anglers want to catch trout during this small window of opportunity using dry flies. The reason? Because it's great fun to watch a trout strike!

Dry flies float on the surface and imitate mayflies, caddis flies, and stoneflies during the part of their life cycle when they are *duns* preparing to take flight. In descending order of importance, dry flies must imitate the size, shape, and color of the real thing as closely as possible. If you're not certain about the size, go smaller. As for shape, look on the water. See what's floating downstream and choose the type of fly accordingly. Lastly, if you have misgivings about color, stick with olive green or brown. Brightly colored flies—like Ernest Hemingway's Yellow Sally—are completely worthless in

Some anglers buy USGS topographical maps to find isolated fishing holes on streams and rivers. They claw their way to these pools only to find rusty beer cans in the streambed. The lesson: Don't try to find spots where no angler has been before; try to find the places with the most trout food!

Sam Tippet Says-

Connecticut waters because trout sense immediately that they are out of place. Always remember that you must use flies that imitate the natural entomology of the place you have chosen.

The first time an angler scoops a Hendrickson dun off the water into his palm, there is a moment of complete confusion, because the real thing and the imitation don't look anything alike. However, imagine a Hendrickson dun flapping its tiny wings so hard it creates a blur—suddenly the imitation makes sense. The dry flies that anglers use are not meant to look exactly like the mayfly on the stream. They are stock-still mimickers of action, and they do a creditable job imitating the real thing. Keep in mind also that trout will snap at leaves, splinters of wood, and almost anything else that floats on a stream.

Depending on who you talk to, the dry fly originated with James Ogden, an English fishing-tackle dealer, who claimed to have used it during the 1840s. However, floating patterns weren't really new at that time. Whether or not Ogden should receive credit for the dry fly is further complicated by the slow acceptance of the patterns. They weren't in general use on the chalk streams of southern

The "Old Stone Bridge" on the West Branch of the Farmington River

England until the late 1880s. And an American, Thaddeus Norris, was using dry flies in the streams around Philadelphia before 1864.

In the ensuing years, the number of different mayfly patterns and hook sizes available to dry-fly anglers has reached the outer limits of reason. Add to the classic patterns of the nineteenth century, the new flies that have been invented down through the years—plus the new patterns that you may have designed by your hearth last winter—and the number of fly patterns becomes a burden. Soon enough, anxiety replaces excitement as the angler despairs that he has not brought the exact right dry fly for the day and stream in question.

The remedy? Invest your confidence in the patterns that have stood the test of time, and cast a jaundiced eye on patterns that are the "latest and greatest." Keep it simple. The most popular dry fly patterns of 1938, Adams, Blue Dun, Light Cahill, Gray Wulff, Dark Hendrickson, and the Quill Gordon are still in use today, and obviously appeal to our fly connoisseurs.

It should come as a welcome surprise for the would-be angler that trout are not geniuses. They do have plenty of native instincts, but it is not uncommon to find many anglers on a given stream catching trout on many different types of dry flies. This is because trout are attracted to the mayfly of the moment, but may just as easily go for a Mosquito, a

Fill a glass with water and then dump a couple of dry flies in to see how they float. The hook faces down and the fly rests on the hackles and the tail. Keep this in mind. If you cannot get your dry flies to float this way out on the river, there's not much chance you will catch trout. When folks talk about the leader rolling over nicely, this is what they mean. If the leader rolls over properly, your dry fly will float on the waters of a trout stream the same way it floats in a glass of water.

Sam Tippet Says-

Black Gnat, or a Blue Winged Olive. Lastly, imitations of terrestrials like grasshoppers, black ants, spiders, beetles, and crickets can also be used. Be forewarned, however, land-roving bugs make up only about 1 percent of a trout's annual diet.

The Blue Winged Olive is a great favorite because its hackles and wings are so pale—almost transparent—that it can imitate almost any yellowish olive-bodied dun. Perhaps because the Blue Winged Olive produces such a neutral effect, it is productive for a large chunk of the fishing season.

Keeping It Dry– When novices first begin to fish with dry flies, they come up against an age-old dilemma—keeping the imitation dry enough to float. There are several options here. First, there are loads of floatants on the market designed to keep dry flies from becoming waterlogged. Mucilin is a long-time standby, still held sacred by older anglers. It comes as thick, waxy paste that becomes liquefied as you use it and works very well. A more space-age solution is silicone gel, found in a variety of floatants. And many anglers use Gehrke's Gink, similar to Mucilin, and purported to be environmentally friendly. No matter which floatant you choose, try to keep the solution off your tippet—including the clinch knot at the eye of the fly—because these products are slippery in the liquid form and can cause knots to slip out.

There is one last option that deserves a mention. Since wind is a far better drying agent than sunlight—or almost anything else—a fly fisher can false cast ten times and produce a fly that is suitably dry. The smaller the fly, the better this works. For larger flies simply increase the number of false casts.

Landing the Fly First & Fly Tying

There are two critical skills in expert dry-fly fishing—a delicate presentation and the ability to set the hook.

Personally, I don't think fly-fisher folks should even consider tying flies until they've been fishing for a couple of years. Only after an angler can cast well, execute an acceptable roll cast, and has earned a university degree in streamology, should tying flies be considered. There was a time when tying flies saved money, but with flies now selling for fifty cents or less, those days are gone. The real reason to tie flies is the satisfaction of catching trout on your own handiwork.

Sam Tippet Says—

Assuming that a fly fisherman or fisherwoman has a well-balanced rod, reel, and line, this delicate touch will develop as the angler learns how to cast properly and present the dry fly in an agreeable manner. In *A River Runs Through It*, Norman Maclean writes that (his) father insisted the fly hit the water first, then the leader, and finally the fly line. But that was in the days of the braided-silk fly line. It is a rare fly fisherman or fly fisherwoman who can do this today.

It isn't easy. The fly, due to its shape and weight, encounters more wind resistance than the fly line, so in a free fall, it must necessarily take longer to get to the water. Also, the fly line gets to the destination first, and then begins to drop toward the water. A dry fly must travel the length of the leader before it ends its journey and begins to drop. Since the fly line has the jump on the fly, it's difficult for the fly to beat the line to the water.

If you insist on getting the fly on the water first, here's how: Cast to a spot in the air three feet above where you want your fly to land. As your fly line reaches the end of its run, lift the tip of your rod so the line starts back towards you. This gives the fly time to hit the water first. Try it, but remember that you won't be the last angler who has difficulty accomplishing it.

Sam Tippet Says—

In the end, it doesn't matter. Once your fly is in position, the fish won't care how it got there.

If you can't get a trout to strike your dry fly, allow it to drift downstream until you can lift the fly—and your line—off the water with a quick flick of the wrist. The trick is to keep from spooking the fish. By moving with great stealth, or better yet, keeping still, you can fish in the same spot for hours. Conversely, if you start splashing around, you'll do plenty of hiking and get to see lots of new scenery!

The second skill, setting the hook, is trickier. In terms of speed, a newcomer to the sport is no match for a feeding trout. A trout can take the fly, taste it quickly, and spit it out before the angler gets over the excitement of the strike. With time and practice though, a natural hook-setting skill will develop. Keep your rod to the side—with the tip close to the water—so that your hook-setting movement is telegraphed to the fly. The surface tension of your fly line on the water makes this possible. As an added bonus, trout turn hard after they strike and inadvertently aid in setting the hook.

There are a few physical considerations in dry fly fishing. When an angler is using dry flies, there's more casting involved than with wet flies and nymphs. A smart fly angler knows that the fly is not to be picked up until it is out of the feeding area. Still, even if the dry fly is allowed to float through this all-important section of the river, it must then be picked up and cast again. Beyond that, if the caster is trying to dry the fly using false casts, the volume of casting increases geometrically. Suddenly fly fishing has lost that quiet, lethargic ambience and become quite an active sport. Still doesn't sound like much effort, does it? Well, maybe not if you are using a 7′6″ fiberglass or graphite rod, but what if you're swinging a 9′0″ split bamboo (Tonkin cane) rod all day long? By suppertime, the only thing you'll be able to think about is rotator cuff surgery. So, plan accordingly. For a day-long dry fly session, travel light. Use a short fiberglass or graphite rod, and pace yourself. Take a break now and then.

A second concern is your wading depth. If you stand in only one foot of water all day, you'll be exhausted by sundown. However, if you're up to your waist in water, you'll tire far less because the water pressure of the river will lend support to your body. For the newcomer—particularly young people—deep wading is not always a realistic option though. It limits the space above the water available for the flight of your fly line. A six-foot angler with a 9′0″ rod has an extra three-and-a-half feet of "flight space" over his five-foot counterpart, swinging a 7′6″ rod. This is just one of the little imponderables that will appear as experience sets in. This so-called "flight space" is important because, in order to cast any distance, the line must go down slightly

"Flies aren't tied for fish, but for other anglers." This adage is as old as the rocks in Connecticut's trout streams, but it's true. Very often when a fly gets a little mangy, it makes an excellent imitation of a mayfly during the spinner stage of the cycle. After the female mayfly has deposited her eggs on the water, she eventually floats downstream, giving trout yet another bite to eat. I have caught trout on brand new flies and on flies that should have been discarded long ago. Don't be too quick to dump them when they get a little haggard.

Sam Tippet Says-

on the back cast, and up slightly on the forward cast. Rest assured though, this does not mean that the tallest man or most statuesque woman will catch more trout. Superior knowledge will always win in this competition.

Wet Flies

Most anglers prefer to use dry flies, switching to wet flies as a last resort. This is not because "fishing 'em wet" is such a poor sport, but because dry-fly fishing is so much more fun. When trout make "dainty rings" as they take flies off the surface, they usually are not far under water. With a minimum of effort, they "tip and sip." Sometimes they will drift with an imitation, inspecting it at close range. But if trout were forced to continuously work hard for such small offerings, they would expend far too much energy while feeding.

Wet flies are for catching trout underwater. Technically, the term "wet fly" means only flies that imitate an insect that has drowned or perhaps some green or brown larvae floating downstream—in sum, almost anything small and inactive that a trout might feed on. In recent years, true wet flies have fallen out of favor with anglers who now prefer nymphs. However, since most fly anglers think of flies as either wet or dry, for the purposes of this book, we will lump together wet flies, midges, nymphs, terrestrials, streamers, and bucktails. Following is a quick explanation of each.

Wet flies imitate dead insects or larvae.

Midges are tiny—sometimes almost microscopic—insects and bugs that are abundant in very slow current and encompass all sorts of tiny life forms. The number of different midges is so hopelessly large, an angler would never be able to learn them all. Suffice it to say, midges are very small and tied on hooks that are size #22 and smaller.

Nymphs imitate mayflies, caddis flies, and stoneflies when they are in the *nymphal* stage of their life cycles. Usually a nymph is fished right below the surface, but in colder weather—when trout are sluggish—nymphs must be fished deeper.

Terrestrials are tied to replicate insects that live on the land—ants and grasshoppers being the most prominent members of this group. There are all sorts of caterpillars and wooly worms that find their way into trout streams, although they are designed to spend their whole lives on land.

Streamers and **bucktails** imitate minnows or sculpin. Streamers are tied with feathers; bucktails with hair. One famous streamer, the Hornberg, is tied using mallard flank feathers and jungle cock feathers over a silver tinsel body. Among the most popular of the bucktails is the Muddler Minnow. Originally tied to represent the Mottled Sculpin, it is now used widely in the Northeast to represent a wide variety of minnows. A Muddler Minnow employs mottled turkey feathers, gold tinsel for the body, and squirrel's tail and spun deer's hair for the wings and head. As you've probably figured out, some streamers and bucktails are a lively combination of feathers *and* hair.

Obviously, an angler should try to use a wet fly or nymph that is appropriate to the season. If it is the beginning of May and a Hendrickson mayfly hatch came off the water earlier in the day, use a Hendrickson nymph. If in doubt, go with any type of a caddis nymph, which imitates larvae or drowned insects.

One big difference between fishing with dry flies and wet flies is the length of leader employed. When fishing under water, use the shortest leader possible. Depending on the clarity of the water, this might mean anything from a 7′-6″ leader on down. When the water is discolored—perhaps because high water is scrubbing soil from the banks—you could drop to a 4-foot leader without fear of spooking leader-wary trout. All in all though, the most popular leader for "fishin' 'em wet" is a 6-footer.

Above all else, the wet-fly angler wants to create a *natural drift* with his imitation. This is accomplished by casting the line directly across the stream and then allowing it to work its way downstream with the flow. All the while, the line should be slack—yet very near taught. If the line isn't slack, there is no chance for a natural drift; yet if the angler doesn't have enough control of the line, he won't be able to feel a trout strike.

After the line is straight out and downriver from you, use your empty hand to gather up the line a few inches at a time using the *hand flop* method of retrieval. The hand flop is easy enough to learn. With your free hand, take the line between your thumb and forefinger, and slowly flop your hand on its back with your palm up and your last three fingers outstretched. Then close them, pinning the line to your palm. Repeat this process, pinning any new line retrieved with the same three fingers.

With wet flies, it is especially important to end the drift and recast from a point where trout are unlikely to be holding. Make sure not to alert trout of your presence by picking up your line in the middle of a pool or some other section of the river favorable to trout. When using wet flies, keep in mind that the angler who imitates a natural drift and keeps his fly in the water the longest will always get the best results.

Another thing to note while fishing with wet flies is your position in relation to the sun. Try to position yourself so that the sun is at your back. Not only will this make it easier for you to see the fly, but it decreases the chance that the trout will see you. Any glare on the water between you and your quarry is an added bonus.

Don't be afraid to strip out more line and allow your fly to drift farther downstream. Sometimes your original length of line will have been used up just as your fly reaches a really promising stretch of water. By creatively stripping

Fishing a nice pool below a culvert

out some extra line, you can play this new stretch without recasting, and thereby help to ensure that your wet fly floats naturally through an extra stretch of the stream.

Along the same lines, while you are using the hand flop method, stop for ten or fifteen seconds every now and then, to let your fly sink back to the bottom—or to whatever depth you feel is most productive in the waters you are working.

There are several ways to keep flies down deep in the water. Some anglers resort to weighted flies while others simply put a piece of split shot on the leader. Both of these methods work—sometimes—but the wet-fly angler will get into a lot less trouble by avoiding lead weights of any kind. Casting with a piece of split shot on your leader isn't easy—and definitely not for the beginner. This added weight changes the way the fly line sinks in the water and, more importantly, *might* suggest a strike when the tug is only the weight sinking in the water. In short, a sinker introduces confusion when every little tug of your line must be understood.

When using a piece of spit shot with a streamer or bucktail, place the shot on the leader right at the eye of the hook. This will make it easier to cast and also give the fly a more natural look in the water. When the split shot is attached away from the imitation minnow, say three feet, each time the angler strips the line, the split shot drops again in the water, giving the "minnow" an unnatural follow up glide after each darting motion. Again, imagination is essential to good fly fishing. You must learn to envision what your minnow looks like as it darts around underwater.

In "fishin' 'em wet," the way you handle your presentation depends greatly on whether you are using a wet fly, a nymph, a stonefly, a streamer, or a bucktail. The wet fly should be naturally floated—as detailed above—as if it were being washed downstream by the current. Stoneflies and nymphs should be brought in patiently using the hand flop method, and can be extremely effective when fishing the riffles. (Riffles, remember, are areas of foot-deep water that flows over a washboard of small rocks.) Streamers and bucktails require an up-and-back motion that causes the hairs to spread out and then immediately flatten on the body of the hook. Some bucktails—like the Muddler Minnow—should be brought in by stripping the line quickly in eighteen-inch sections—with the rod tip held low to imitate the way a minnow darts around in the water. In each case, the angler must use his imagination to make sure the imitation behaves naturally. It's uncanny the way even hatchery-raised trout can distinguish between the real thing and an imitation.

Sam Tippet Says-

In every type of fly fishing, you should get into the habit of seeing how long it takes for wet flies to sink to the bottom, and so forth. Like all living things, trout establish feeding rhythms, and to the extent that an angler understands this, he will be successful or endure some mighty long days.

Any angler can quickly make a nymph that imitates a caterpillar or grub out of an old dry fly by simply trimming the hackles on a dry fly and then using it as a wet fly. Just as there is no perfect human being, there is no perfect insect, bug, caterpillar, ant, 'hopper, mosquito, spider, or grub. Don't be afraid to go with what you have and use your developing presentation skills to fool a trout into saying "yes."

Among the fraternity of anglers, there are what might be called specialists—those who choose exclusively midges and others who employ only nymphs. Since trout do almost all of their feeding beneath the surface, there is a certain simple logic to this. However, these specialists have chosen to spend their whole lives on trout streams without ever experiencing the excitement of a large rainbow trout surfacing to strike at their Light Cahill or Ginger Quill. One can't help but admire the dedication of this austere persuasion, but to join them is another matter. For most anglers, the thrill is in the rise.

Chapter 8
Finding Fish

The Connecticut DEP—Inland Fisheries Division offers all the information you need to find your way to legal fishing spots in Connecticut. Use their web site for the most up-to-date information. (See "A Few Recommended Web Sites" on page 100).

Lodging

True, fly fishing is what it's all about, but don't overlook how much the angling experience can be enhanced by a stay at a comfortable lodge with a great dining room. Too often, anglers race to their favorite trout stream, fish for a couple of hours and then speed home. But with an overnight stay, an angler can get in a full weekend of fishing with all meals and lodging provided at a reasonable price. This method turns fly fishing into a whole different sport.

Here is a sampling of Connecticut B & Bs where anglers are more than welcome.

West Branch–Farmington River

Old Riverton Inn

436 East River Road (P.O. Box 6), Riverton, CT 06065
Tel: 860-379-8678 or toll free 800-378-1796
Email: innkeeper@rivertoninn.com
Innkeepers: Mark and Pauline Telford

The Old Riverton Inn overlooks the wild and scenic West Branch of the Farmington River.

West Branch–Farmington River

Pine Meadow House B & B
398 Main Street, Pine Meadow, CT 06061
Tel: 860-379-8745
Email: prossmanfly@charter.net
Innkeepers: Paul Rossman & Cheri Clay

The Pine Meadow House B & B sits right below the Trout Management Area on the West Branch of the Farmington River.

Housatonic River

Breadloaf Mountain Lodge & Cabins
13 Route 7, Cornwall Bridge, CT 06754
Telephone: 860-672-6064 or 860-672-6709
Email: info@breadloafmountainlodge.com
Innkeeper: Martin Iannone

Bread Loaf Mountain sits on the banks of the Housatonic River.

Quinebaug & Shetucket Rivers

Lathrop Manor B & B
380 Washington Street
Norwich, CT 06360
Tel: 860-204-9448
Email: innkeeper@lathropmanor.com
Innkeepers: Sheryl and Marco Middleton

Lathrop Manor is only about six miles from the lower ends of the Quinebaug and Shetucket Rivers.

Quinebaug River

Branch Place B & B
34 Newent Rd.
Lisbon, Connecticut, 06351-2925
Tel: (860) 376-5885; (866) 376-5885
Email: branchplace@comcast.net
Innkeeper: Ethel and Tom Bosse

The Quinebaug River is only two miles to the east of the Branch Place B & B, and the Shetucket and Merrick Rivers are a little further to the west.

Quinebaug River

Lonesome Dove B & B
332 South Burnham Hwy
Lisbon, Ct. 06351
Tel: 860-859-9600; 877-793-9880
Email: macdore@sbcglobal.net
Innkeepers: Ruth and Leo MacDonald

Only a short distance away from the Lonesome Dove
B & B are a number of good trout stream including the
Quinebaug, Shetucket and Merrick Rivers.

Camping

There are also plenty of campgrounds throughout the State
of Connecticut that are within prime distance to excellent
fishing spots. Here are a few of the more popular spots:

AMERICAN LEGION STATE FOREST
The Austin Hawes Campground is open for the season
from April 15 through October 10 (daily).
- West River Road, Pleasant Valley
- Austin F. Hawes Memorial Campground, midway
  between Pleasant Valley and Riverton on West
  River Road. 30 sites in pine woods. Dumping
  station, bathrooms, showers, fishing. No swimming.
  One pet/site permitted. Reservations accepted
  April 20 through Columbus Day.
- Campground Office (860) 379-0922
- Forest Headquarters (860) 379-2469

HOPEVILLE POND STATE PARK
Hopeville Pond Campground is open for the season from
April 16 through September 30 (daily).
193 Roode Road, Jewett City
- 80 wooded sites near pond. Concession, dumping
  station, bathrooms, showers. Fishing, swimming.
  No pets.
- Campground Office (860) 376-0313
- Park Office (860) 376-2920

HOUSATONIC MEADOWS STATE PARK

The Housatonic Meadows Campground is open for the season from April 15 through October 10 (daily).

- Route 7, Sharon
- 95 sites in rustic setting near Housatonic River. Dumping station, bathrooms, showers.
  No swimming. No pets.
- Alcohol-free campground. Please do not bring alcoholic beverages.
- Campground Office (860) 672-6772
- Park Office (860) 927-3238

MACEDONIA BROOK STATE PARK

Macedonia Brook Campground is open for the season from April 15 through September 30 (daily).

- 159 Macedonia Brook Road, Kent
- 51 sites in rustic setting. Stream fishing, excellent hiking, no swimming. No pets. Reservations accepted April 20 through Labor Day.
- Alcohol-free campground. Please do not bring alcoholic beverages.
- Campground Office (860) 927-4100
- Park Office (860) 927-3238

NATCHAUG STATE FOREST

- Pilfershire Road, Eastford
- Silvermine Horse Camp. 15 wooded sites.
  Basic facilities only—campers are responsible for cleaning sites and carrying out all trash.
  Pet permitted.
  No fee.
- Tel: (860) 974-1562

Guide Services

The reason that legendary fly fishermen always caught fish was because they hired guides. When the artist Winslow Homer fished the Adirondacks with his brother Charles, they hired guides—thus, the famous watercolor *Adirondack Guide*. Our fly-fishing presidents—Coolidge, Hoover, Eisenhower, and Carter—all had guides to get them to the trout. Even the renowned fly fisherman Joe Brooks used to hire guides like Lefty Kreh.

There is no shame in hiring a guide to help you with your casting and bring you to the best spots on an unfamiliar trout stream. In Connecticut, there are guide services available at fishing outfitters near most of the major trout streams. Here are a few leads:

- Antoine Bissieux; Tel: 860-759-4464,
  email: bissieux@msn.com

- Marla Blair's Fly Fishing Guide Service &
  Instruction: 18 Letendre Ave. Ludlow, MA 01056;
  Tel: 413-583-5141 (Fax- same number);
  Email: marlablair@yahoo.com

- Shawn F. Britton; Tel: 860-309-8588;
  email: Bootroutman@gmail.com

- Housatonic Anglers: 26 Bolton Hill Rd.,
  Cornwall, CT 06753; Tel: 860-672-4457

- Housatonic Meadows Fly Shop, 13 Rte. 7,
  Cornwall Bridge, CT 06754; Tel: 860-672-6064

- Housatonic River Outfitters: 24 Kent Rd.,
  Cornwall Bridge, CT 06754; Tel: 860-672-1010

- Sara Low Fly Fishing; Tel: 401-447-6462;
  Email: hoopsnflies@msn.com

Chapter 9
Cooking Your Catch

Since some anglers do cook and eat trout rather than catch and release, a couple of proven recipes might come in handy. Keep in mind that there are four ways to cook trout—fry, bake, boil or broil. Herewith, some worthwhile recipes:

When dressing a trout, leave the heads and tails in place. Slit the belly from stem to stern with a sharp knife, pull out the innards and toss them into the garbage, bury them away from camp, or toss them into the campfire, depending on regulations in the area.

"Dress" is gourmet lingo meaning "prepare."

Pan Fried Trout— # 1 (in camp)

Since trout have tiny scales, they are the perfect fish to dress and then roll in yellow corn meal—or your choice of flour, like wheat, quinoa, chickpea or almond—just enough to thinly coat, and sauté in butter or olive oil. This is the most common way to cook trout around the campfire. Trout cook best in a heavy-bottomed skillet over a low steady heat, so don't be in a hurry. Ideally, you'll want the meat cooked through and the exterior nice and brown. Be sure to add extra butter or olive oil in the cooking process as needed. If you know your wild edibles, add some chopped wood sorrel, wild onion or other stronger tasting herbs to the cooked fish. Serve while still piping hot.

Truite Canadienne (baked in camp)

Dress your trout leaving the heads and tails intact. Rub the inside of the fish with butter or olive oil and sprinkle with salt and pepper. Place the trout in the center of a large square of aluminum foil (leaving ample room on all sides). Cut some orange slices and arrange on each fish. Wrap tightly, and lay the packet in a bed of hot coals for about 15 minutes. It doesn't get any easier and the orange slices do wonders with the trout.

Baked Trout with Vegetables (in camp)

This is an easy way to serve trout in camp with vegetables. Again, dress the trout in the usual way, leaving the heads and tails in place. Season with salt, pepper and lemon juice. (Add other herbs as desired). Dice up small some carrots, onions, garlic—and any other vegetables you brought along—and toss. Fill the gut cavity of the trout with this vegetable mix (you will want about 1/3 cup vegetable mix per fish) and tightly wrap the stuffed fish in tinfoil. Place the foil-wrapped trout on a bed of hot coals for 15-20 minutes. Carefully remove one packet from the coals and test for doneness. Either return to the heat or remove the rest of the fish, and serve on a bed of brown rice.

Truite Bleue (boiled at home)

    4 bullion cubes plus 1 quart water
      or 1 quart of strong vegetable stock
    1 bay leaf
    1 tablespoon minced onion
    2 sprigs parsley
    2 pinches dried thyme or a sprig of fresh thyme
    tips from one stalk of celery
    4-5 peppercorns
    ½ cup white vinegar
    ¾ cup of white wine
    about four good-sized trout

Dress the trout in the usual way, leaving the heads and tails in place. Make a court bullion in a skillet, using the bullion cubes and water or your own stock. Add in everything but the vinegar and wine. Simmer. Meanwhile, boil ½ cup of white vinegar and carefully pour it over the trout. Then discard the vinegar. Now, turn up the heat under the stock. When it's back to a boil, add the wine and carefully place the trout into the pot. The fish will cook in only a few minutes. Remove with a large slotted spoon and serve with salted lemon butter or a good olive oil drizzled on top.

Baked Stuffed Trout with Bacon (baked at home)

Dress the trout in the usual way, leaving the heads and tails in place. Stuff the cavity with your favorite stuffing—bread and celery, bread and oysters, bread and crabmeat or perhaps mushrooms and wild rice. There are plenty of possibilities. Close the belly with small clamps, or tie with string. Place the fish in a well-greased oven pan and lay a few strips of bacon over them. Season as you wish and then cook about 12 minutes per pound in a 375° oven. (For 10" to 12" trout, 350° for 40 minutes works fine.) Baste with the juices as it cooks. Serve.

Broiled Trout (at home)

Dress the usual way, leaving the heads and tails. Lightly cover the bottom of an oven pan with melted butter, olive oil, peanut oil, or sesame oil, and seasoning (to your taste). Sprinkle a thin layer of breadcrumbs over the seasoned oil and lay in the trout. Turn once and place under the broiler. After the fish are broiled to a golden brown, set the oven to bake at 450° and cook fish for 5 minutes more. Serve with your choice of side dishes.

Sam Tippet Says-

Of course, if you are like me, you release your trout after the thrill of the catch. So, what do I cook at camp you ask? Try this fun recipe. It'll feed you and your partner.

Pinto Bean Tamales for Hungry Catch-And-Release Anglers

18 green or dried cornhusks
a pot of boiling water
12 eight inch pieces of string
1 16oz can of refried beans
¼ cup cornmeal
1 cup (total) diced vegetables of your choice (onions, peppers, chiles, mushrooms, greens, celery, corn, or whatever you are in the mood for)
1 TBS olive oil
1 six ounce can tomato paste
2 teaspoons chili powder
a pinch of salt
2 to 2 1/2 cups water

Place cornhusks in boiling water just long enough to soften; drain and pat dry. Alternatively, you can soak your cornhusks in warm water for about an hour; drain and pat dry.

Sauté the vegetables in the olive oil until just tender. Don't overcook. Mix the cornmeal with the refried beans.

For each tamale: Lay three overlapping cornhusks on a flat surface. Spread about 1/3 cup bean mixture on the center husk leaving about 2 inches space from the top and bottom. Spoon about 2 tablespoons of your vegetable mixture down the center of the beans. Carefully lift the sides of the other two cornhusks to encourage the beans to surround the vegetables. Now, continue rolling the cornhusks to fully enclose your bean and vegetable bundle. Tie ends securely with string. Your tamales should resemble ears of corn.

In a large skillet, combine tomato paste, chili powder, salt and 2 cups water. Bring to a boil. Carefully place a single layer of tamales in sauce, cover and simmer for 20 to 30 minutes. Lift out cooked tamales with tongs or a slotted spoon. Depending on the size of your skillet, repeat until all six tamales are cooked adding more water if needed. Serve in husks, open and enjoy with a side of rice.

An Angler's Glossary

action – the physical characteristics of a fly rod—particularly with regard to its stiffness and movement in casting.

angler – a person who fishes.

aquatic insect – an insect that is hatched under water.

arbor – the central spool of a fishing reel. Fly-fishing reels are now available with small, medium and large arbors.

arbor knot – a special knot used to attach backing or fly-fishing line to the arbor of a reel.

backing material – inexpensive extra line used to bulk up a fly-fishing reel before the fly line is added. Fly-fishing reels with medium or large arbor eliminate the need for backing.

bait fish – smaller fish—especially minnows—used to catch bigger fish.

bank – the shorelines of a river, stream or lake.

barb – a sharp opposing prong on a hook that ensures that a fish cannot "spit the hook."

barbless hook – a hook without a barb. These hooks are preferred anytime trout are destined to be released. To make a barbless hook out of one with a barb, pinch the barb flat with a small pair of pliers.

brackish water – a fresh and saltwater mix; any fresh water with a salty taste.

breaks off – when a trout breaks an angler's tippet and gets away.

brood stock – larger trout—previously used as breeders—stocked by the Inland Fisheries Division.

bucktail – a fly tied almost exclusively with hair, used to imitate small minnows and bait fish.

caddis fly – aquatic insect with delicate antennae, which project forward. Caddis flies' wings are covered with fine hair, are four in number and are carried tent-like when at rest. Most frequently, caddis flies are dull gray or brown.

catch-and-release – methodology used in releasing fish after the catch. This phrase is also used to indicate areas, like Trout Management Areas, where regulations require fish to be released.

channel – deeper section of a stream or pool where the main current passes.

char – Any of several fishes related to the trout and salmon. Although brook trout are almost universally referred to as trout, they are actually a member of the char family.

creel limit – number of fish that can be taken in a day.

crustacean – an aquatic species characteristically having a segmented body, a hard outer shell and paired, jointed limbs.

current – the part of a body of water moving continuously in a certain direction. Also sometimes used to refer to the swiftest part of a stream.

damselfly – one of the five insects of a wholly aquatic habitat— along with caddis flies, mayflies, stone flies and dragonflies. Damselflies are similar to dragonflies but smaller. They drape their wings over their backs at rest.

dapping – method of dangling a fly over a rock or riverbank usually with only the leader, tippet, and fly touching the water. Dapping can be especially effective in "seams" that flowing water forms on the downstream sides of large rocks.

dead-drift – Often referred to as a natural drift. When your fly floats downstream—drag-free—at the same pace as the current of the stream or river.

disk-drag – a disk-drag reel allows you to apply more or less tension to a fly line by turning the drag control knob on the reel.

double taper – type of fly line that is flat along most of its length, but tapered on the last fifteen feet of each end.

drag – 1. mechanical devise inside a fly reel that restrains the fly line as it pays out; 2. when your fly is pulled out of a natural drift. (See dead-drift.)

dragonfly – insects that are larger and stouter—and more predatory—than damselflies. Dragonflies hold their wings horizontal in repose.

dress – clean or prepare a fish for cooking.

dressing – the hairs, feathers, hackle, dubbing, thread and hooks used to tie flies. The materials used to tie flies adds up to an almost endless list, but the items mentioned above are the most common components.

drift – *See* dead-drift.

dry fly – any of hundreds of artificial flies tied to float on the surface of the water.

dun – the stage in the development of a mayfly where the "emerger" dries its wings and takes flight.

eddy – the term used when water hits an obstruction in its flow and actually reverses direction. In fast moving water, eddies don't last long, as the current forces the water downstream soon enough.

emerger/emergent – the stage in the development of mayflies, and other aquatic insects, where a nymph moves to the surface of the water to become a "dun."

false cast – anytime a fly fisher cats his line back and forth—to better align a cast or to dry a fly.

ferrule joint – on a fly rod, the male and female metal parts that allow the rod to be pulled apart for storage.

fingerling – a small, immature trout.

floatant – a paste, liquid, or spray, used to treat a dry fly so that it will float.

fly – any of hundreds of dressed hooks tied to imitate a natural insect, worm, or minnow.

guides – the loops on a fly rod used to pay out the fly line.

hand flop – method of slowly retrieving a wet fly line. Sometimes called "hand twist."

hatch – when mayflies—or other insects—turn from emergers to duns and take flight off the water.

haul – a technique used to lengthen a cast. The single haul and the double haul will have to be learned over time, but are not essential at the start of a fly-fishing career.

hemostat – surgical tongs used to take a hook from a trout's mouth or throat.

hookup – result of a fish's strike and the setting of the hook.

hydrography – the study of the flow of streams.

shank – the long, straight section of a hook.

keeper – small wire loop just ahead of the grip on a fly rod and used to hook a fly when not in use.

knotless leader – a tapered leader that does not have many small sections of monofilament tied together with blood knots.

larva – the immature, wingless, sometime wormlike feeding form that hatches from the eggs of many insects.

leader – the monofilament between the fly line and the tippet. About 90 percent of the leaders used today are of the tapered variety, eliminating the need for tying together small pieces of monofilament used to make a knotted leader.

leader straightener – a piece of rubber or leather used to take the "memory" out of a leader that has been kept coiled on a reel.

Mayfly – an aquatic insect with a nymph stage and a short-lived adult stage. Mayflies have membranous wings and two or three long caudal styles.

mending – method of flipping the central body of an outstretched fly line upstream to give a fly more drag-free floating time.

midge – small gnat-like aquatic insects.

monofilament – a single strand of untwisted synthetic line.

natural drift – *See* dead drift.

nipper – a devise resembling a nail clipper used to clip monofilament.

nymph – an aquatic insect during its underwater immature stage.

nymphing – name given to the type of fishing where the bait used imitate the nymphal stage of aquatic insects.

pattern – the imitation (fly) of a natural insect.

pocket water – name given to the quiet water behind a rock, log or other natural obstruction in a stream or river.

pool – a barely moving, deep stretch of water in a stream or river.

reel – circular devise used to roll up the fly line and leader.

riffle – the washboard-looking section of a stream or river where shallow water moves quickly over a fairly uniform bed of small rocks.

rise – when a fish breaks the surface of the water to grab a natural insect or imitation fly.

redd – a crater dug in sand and gravel by a female trout preparing a nest for her eggs.

roll cast – a cast that does not employ a back cast. The roll cast is essential in areas where a back cast is not possible because of rocks, trees and other natural obstructions.

roll over – the process by which the leader, tippet and fly float nicely on the water in a predictable and linear fashion.

run – 1. smooth stretch of water on a river or stream. 2. the back and forth racing of a fish after being hooked.

sculpin – small bottom-feeding fish with sharp spines instead of scales.

seam – place on a stream where quiet water and fast moving water meet. Trout love to pick insects out of these areas.

skunk – when the fish wins. To outsmart the angler, and not get caught.

spawn – mating of fish. Rainbow trout spawn in the spring. Browns and brook trout spawn in the fall.

spent – the condition of a female spinner after she lays her eggs on the water.

spinner – 1. mayfly reproductive stage. 2. an imitation fly that attempts to match this stage of the mayfly life cycle.

split shot – tiny balls of lead with a slit across the center so they can be attached to monofilament.

spook – to scare fish into hiding.

spool – inner circular metal devise upon which the fly line wraps —either with backing added first or with no backing at all.

stonefly – a primitive aquatic insect with a flattened body.

streamer – fly pattern used to imitate minnows, sculpin and other small bait fish. Streamers are tied almost exclusively with feathers.

streamology – knowledge of the critical elements of a trout stream—what and where the trout food is, where the trout are, and what will it take to catch them.

strike – when a fish takes an angler's fly.

strip – the act of pulling line off a reel.

tail water – the water below a natural or man-made dam.

terrestrials – land-based insects that would not ordinarily be found in a trout stream. Grasshoppers, mosquitoes, beetles, crickets, ants are the most common members of this group. A fly fisher should always remember that only 1 percent of a trout's annual diet is terrestrials.

tippet – very fine monofilament that connects the end of the leader with the fly.

void – defecate.

waders – rubber or synthetic booted pants worn by anglers (and hunters) to keep dry.

wading staff – a pole used by anglers to make wading easier and safer.

wet fly – pattern used to imitate insects floating below the surface of the water. Although traditionally wet flies were only flies that imitate dead insects or larvae, most anglers consider flies either wet or dry. This puts midges, nymphs, terrestrials, bucktails and streamers into the wet fly category.

zinger – button-like devise with a thin retractable cord used to hold nippers and hemostats. It is worn pinned to a fishing vest.

Acknowledgements

As usual, I must recognize the great debt that I owe my parents, Bob and Mary Murphy for giving me life, a solid education and a million incidentals along the way.

I'd also like to extend a warm thank you to the Director of the Inland Fisheries Division of Connecticut, Peter Aarrestad, for his many and varied contributions. In the same vein, I am indebted to Inland Fisheries Division Biologists Neal Hagstrom and Anthony Petrillo, whose help was continuous and much needed.

On the publishing side, I will always owe a huge debt to Director and Editor-in-chief of Wesleyan University Press, Suzanna Tamminen, who ceaselessly extends herself to hapless writers like me; to Leslie Starr the Assistant Director and Marketing Manager, who continues to be a good friend and sounding board; Parker Smathers, whose patience and courtesy continue to confound me; and to Stephanie Elliott, the unsung but hard working publicist of the outfit. Victoria Stahl, one of the finest editor I know, also deserves singular praise.

The staff at the Connecticut Historical Society was helpful and cheerful as usual—Kate Steinberg, Diana McCain, Barbara Austen, Nancy Finlay, Sierra Dixon, Karen DePauw and Richard C. Malley.

At the Connecticut State Library, a word of appreciation goes to Carolyn Picciano, Jeannie Sherman, Mel Smith, Carol Ganz, Bonnie Linck, Steve Rice, Kristi Finnan, Kevin Johnson and Mark Jones for all their help.

An added bit of thanks goes to Duane Raver for allowing me to use his beautiful paintings of trout on the cover of this book, and for his thoughtfulness and help throughout the process.

I'd also like to extend praise and thanks to fellow author and fly fisherman Jay Ford Thurston of Wisconsin for his valuable insight into water temperatures and habitat in trout fishing.

Lastly, a hearty word of appreciation goes to Nancy Burstein and Nick Flynn of Williamstown, Massachusetts, for working so hard to find a photograph of ichthyologist and fly rod maker Reggie Galvin.

This, I'm afraid, is only a representative collection of the people who contributed to *Fly Fishing in Connecticut*. For those I may have inadvertently failed to mention by name, this book is yours too. Many thanks.

Notes

Chapter 1

p.4   "On May 4, 1873, two Hartford men": "Fish and Game,"
Hartford Daily Times, May 5, 1873, 2.

p.4   "rapidly diminishing in number": "A Word More About Shad,"
Hartford Daily Courant, May 25, 1869, 2.

p.4   "shad fishing was nearly used up": "Committee Meetings,"
Hartford Daily Courant, February 21, 1878, 2.

p.4   "the restoration of the salmon": "Legislative Reports," *Hartford
Daily Courant,* May 21, 1872, 1.

p.4   "Other factors include the denuding": Karas, Nick, *Brook Trout,*
(Guilford, CT: Lyons Press, 1997, 2002), 77.

p.5   "each trout the sum of one dollar": "Public Acts," *Hartford Daily
Courant,* July 20, 1861, 2. (Public Acts, Chapter LXXI, An Act
For The Preservation of Game and Fish, Chapter LXXI, Sec. 3.).

p.5   "fish-hatching business in 1872": "Connecticut Legislature,"
Hartford Daily Courant, May 24, 1873, 2.

p.5   "fish were released into the wild": "Propagating Fish," *Hartford
Daily Courant,* October 9, 1902, 3.

p.5   "two million eggs behind their farmhouse": Trumbull, J.
Hammond, *The Memorial History of Hartford County: 1633-1884*
(Boston: Edward L. Osgood, Publisher, 1886), 523.

p.5   "Connecticut waters until a decade later": "Additional State
News," *Hartford Daily Courant,* June 16, 1885, 3.; "State Fish
Commission," *Hartford Courant,*" August 9, 1893, 3.; Gordon,
Theodore, *American Trout Fishing,* (New York: Alfred A. Knopf,
1966), 51.: Karas, 31, 364-65.; "Cold Spring Hatchery,"
New York Times, March 15, 1883, 3.; "Tantalizing To Anglers,"
New York Times, April 2, 1884, 8.

p.5   "to establish a state hatchery": "Additional State News,"
Hartford Daily Courant, June 16, 1885, 3.

p.6   "paid less than $1 a year": "About Trout," *Hartford Daily Courant,*
February 7, 1882, 2.

p.6 "in an eight-gallon can—at no charge": "Fish and Other Foods," *Hartford Daily Courant*, January 10, 1881, 2.; "The Trouting By And By," *Hartford Daily Courant*, April 16, 1880, 2; "The Young Shad," *Hartford Courant*, January 6, 1881, 2. Young shad—originally from Havre de Grace, Maryland—arrived in Connecticut on the Washington train in thirty-gallon cans—each containing 20,000 half-inch shad fry. Simple math shows that 5,000 trout fry would fit into a can of seven to eight gallons of water.

p.6 "released into public rivers and streams": "Windsor," *Hartford Courant*, February 18, 1908, 15.; "The Trouting By And By," *Hartford Daily Courant*, April 16, 1880, 2.; "Hartford & Vicinity," *Hartford Daily Courant*, March 5, 1885, 2.

p.7 "Hathaway Mill on River Street in Poquonock":"Fish and Game," *Hartford Courant*, January 5, 1897, 10.; "Windsor," *Hartford Courant*, February 18, 1908, 15.

p.7 "Game and Fish Warden of Hartford County":"Abbott C. Collins," *Hartford Courant*, April 15, 1902, 13.; "The New Game Law," *Hartford Courant*, August 12, 1889, 8.

p.7 "and then only by hook and line": "Game and Fish Laws," *Hartford Daily Courant*, June 19, 1889, 2.

p.7 "That fall, hatchery employees released": "Game Season Ended," *Hartford Daily Courant*, December 16, 1897, 8.

p.7 "on the Housatonic River below Shelton": "The Raising of Trout," *Hartford Daily Courant*, September 1, 1900, 5.

p.8 "and 15,000 of the land-locked variety": "State Fish Hatcheries," *Hartford Courant*, October 10, 1899, 3. See Author's Note #12 regarding the size of the cans used to ship large numbers of fish fry.

p.8 "hatch out the following spring": "Propagating Fish," *Hartford Courant*, October 9, 1902, 3.

p.9 "within the means of the poorest": "Fish and Other Foods," *Hartford Daily Courant*, January 10, 1881, 2.

p.9 "summer and fall visitors from other states": "Fisheries and Game," *Hartford Courant*, January 9, 1899, 4.

p.9 "for a lobster hatchery at Noank": "Big Trout Killed," *Hartford Courant*, August 1, 1905, 11.

p.9 "hatcheries at South Wareham, Massachusetts": "Trout Breeding in Connecticut," *Hartford Courant*, September 14, 1924, 11.

p.9 "foreman of the facility at Windsor Locks": Ibid; U. S. Census Records, 1920, 1930.

p.9 "source-to-sea cleanups were decades away": "Dwindling Waters Supply Menace To Old Trout Hatchery," *Hartford Courant*, February 18, 1923, 20.

p.10 "dance pavilion at Electric Park in Rockville": "Trout Breeding in Connecticut," *Hartford Courant*, September 14, 1924, 11.

p.10 "from a hatchery on Cape Cod": "Propagating Fish," *Hartford Courant*, October 9, 1902, 3.

p.10 "paid for the state's hatcheries program": "44,671 Angling Licenses Issued," *Hartford Courant*, November 21, 1924, 2.

p.11 "weights and limits to please the fishermen": "The Sportsman's Friend: Dr. Russell P. Hunter Directs Huge Fish and Game Program for the State," *Hartford Courant*, October 14, 1951, SM7.

p.11 "U.S. Fish and Wildlife Service supplied": "State Hatcheries Fill Modern Needs," *Hartford Courant*, July 12, 1970, 17M.

p.11 "time to erect another hatchery": "Here Come The Trout," *Hartford Courant*, April 9, 1972, 2J.

p.12 "biggest fish hatchery east of the Mississippi": Ibid.; "Water Problems To Cut State's Trout Supply," *Hartford Courant*, January 24, 1984, A1.

p.13 "trout fishing is on the wane":

p.13 "taken a toll on the streams and rivers": Karas, 77-85, 225-26, 337-42. "Lake Clear Hatchery Hurting, Trout Stocking Going Down," *Adirondack Daily Enterprise*, November 19, 2010, n.p. This newspaper article includes the following paragraph, "The total recommended staffing levels to maintain sufficient production is 80 persons. Unfilled vacancies over the past few years and additional staff losses resulting from the early retirement incentive have left a skeleton fish culture crew of 67 people. This level of staffing is insufficient to maintain production for stocking of fish into the streams and lakes of New York."; "Fish Stocking To Drop In Spring," *Adirondack Daily Enterprise*, November 23, 2010, n.p.

p.13 "stocking about half as many trout": Vermont Fish & Wildlife Department, Batten Kill Trout Management Plan 2007–2012 at http://www.vtfishandwildlife.com/fisheries_battenkill. cfm (accessed February 25, 2011). Two paragraphs from the report follow: "The final management plan, approved by Fish & Wildlife Commissioner Wayne Laroche, was amended and focuses squarely on restoring habitat required by the river's wild trout populations with the goal of rebuilding the trout fishery. There are no plans to stock trout into the river within the term of the six-year plan, 2007–2012. Over the past half dozen years, the department and other agencies have conducted numerous studies to identify likely causes for the reduced abundance of wild brown in the Batten Kill," said department fisheries biologist, Ken Cox. "Results from these investigations point to habitat deficiencies that have been in the making for many years and more recently reached a critical tipping point." Vermont Fish & Wildlife Department, 2010 Stocking Schedule at http://www.vtfishandwildlife.com/fish_stocking.cfm (accessed February 25, 2011); Connecticut is 5,544 square miles while Vermont is 9,615.

Chapter 2

p.16 "the finest trout brooks in the world": "Fish Culture," *Hartford Daily Courant*, July 30, 1880, 2.

p.19 "is financially out of the question": Telephone Interview with Inland Fisheries Division Senior Biologist Neil Hagstrom. December 15, 2010.

Chapter 4

p.37 "of the classic Wheatley design": "The History of Richard Wheatley Fly Boxes: From the Notes of Richard's Grandson-Frank Wheatley," at http://www.anglersportgroup.com/data/ MiscPDF/Wheatley%20history.pdf (accessed April 14, 2011).

Chapter 7

p.67 "around Philadelphia before 1864": Wright, Leonard M., Jr. and Allen, Gordon, *Field & Stream Treasury of Trout Fishing*, (Guilford: Globe-Pequot Press, 2004), 140.; Norris, Thaddeus, *The American Angler's Book*, (Philadelphia: E. H. Butler & Co., 1864), 312-322.

A Few Recommended Web Sites

http://www.ct.gov . . . The State of Connecticut's official website. In the search box type "fishing" or "DEP, Inland Fisheries Division" to find permits, licenses, stocking reports, hatcheries, or any other information that you may need.

http://www.fws.gov/northeast/ct.htm . . . Homepage for the Connecticut Coordinator's Office of the U.S. Fish and Wildlife Services.

http://www.amff.com . . . The American Museum of Fly Fishing in Manchester, Vermont. Take a look at some of the fly-fishing gear used by Ernest Hemingway, Winslow Homer, Ted Williams, Dwight Eisenhower, and a host of other anglers.

http://www.ctriver.org . . . The Connecticut River Watershed Council. See this site for Source to Sea Cleanups and other ways to be involved in keeping Connecticut's water clean and safe, and its fish happy.

http://www.cttrout.org . . . Trout Unlimited's Connecticut Council. Committed to "conserving, restoring, and preserving North America's coldwater fisheries and their watersheds," Trout Unlimited is a national grassroots organization with eight chapters in the state. Find your local chapter at http://www.cttrout.org/localchapters.html.

http://www.tu.org/about-us/youth . . . Trout Unlimited's Headwaters Youth Education Initiative, including youth education and outreach activities such as "Stream Explorers": http://www.streamexplorers.org.

http://water.usgs.gov . . . The U.S. Geological Survey's information on the nation's water resources. Use the drop-down menu to get USGS real-time water data for Connecticut.

http://ctrivers.wikispaces.com/ . . . The Connecticut Rivers Wiki is "for anyone interested in Connecticut's waterways."

Fly Fishing Canon

Bergman, Ray. *TROUT*. New York: Alfred A. Knopf, 1962.

Dick, Lenox. *The Art & Science of Fly fishing*. New York: Winchester Press, 1972.

Evanoff, Vlad (editor). *Fishing Secrets of the Experts*. Garden City, New York: Doubleday & Company, 1962.

Evanoff, Vlad. *Another 1001 Fishing Tips and Tricks*. New York: Harper & Row, 1970.

Farmington River Anglers Association. *A Guide to Fishing the Farmington River*, 1992.

Fuller, Tom. *Trout Streams of Southern New England: An Angler's Guide to the Watersheds of Massachusetts, Connecticut, and Rhode Island*. Woodstock, VT: Backcountry Guides, 1999.

Gingrich, Arnold. *The Fishing in Print*. New York: Winchester Press, 1974.

Goodwin, Mike. *Trout Streams of Eastern Connecticut: A Guide to the Streams East of the Connecticut River*. Trout Unlimited–Thames Valley Chapter, 2004.

Gordon, Theodore. *American Trout Fishing*. New York: Alfred A. Knopf, 1966.

Karas, Nick. *Brook Trout*. Guilford, CT: The Lyons Press, 1997, 2002.

Kreh, Lefty. *101 Fly-fishing Tips: Practical Advise from a Master Angler*. New York: Lyons Press, 2000.

———. *Lefty Kreh's Ultimate Guide to Fly Fishing: Everything Anglers Need to Know by the World's Foremost Fly-fishing Expert*. New York: Lyons Press, 2003.

Leonard, J. Edson. *Flies*. New York: A. S. Barnes & Co., 1950.

Maclean, Norman. *A River Runs Through It*. Chicago: University of Chicago Press, 1976.

McClane, A. J. *The Compleat McClane: A Treasury of A. J. McClane's Classic Angling Adventures.* New York: Truman Talley Books, 1988.

Meade, Tom. Essential Fly Fishing. New York: Lyons & Burford, 1994.

Meyer, Jerry. *How to Catch Trout Between the Hatches.* New York: Charles Scribner's Sons, 1982.

Norris, Thaddeus. *American Angler's Book.* Philadelphia: Porter & Coates, 1864.

Ovington, Ray. *The Trout and the Fly.* New York: Hawthorne Books, 1977.

Sampson, Bob. *Best Fishing Trips in Connecticut from Ponds to Pounding Surf.* Wilton, CT: Perry Heights Press, 2004.

Trench, Charles Chenevix. *A History of Angling.* Chicago: Follett Publishing Co., 1974.

Wright, Leonard M., Jr. *Fly-Fishing Heresies.* New York: Winchester Press, 1975.

Wulff, Lee. *Fishing with Lee Wulff.* New York: Alfred Knopf, 1972.

————. *Trout on a Fly.* New York: Nick Lyons Books, 1986.

Illustration Credits

All drawings and illustrations in this book are done by the author.

Photographs

Page 6 – Kettle Brook Hatchery. Photograph copied from the *Third Biennial Report of the State Commissioners of Fisheries and Game, 1899–1900*, Hartford: From the press of Hartford Printing Company, Elihu Geer & Sons, 1900, frontispiece. These reports are in bound volumes at the Connecticut State Library, Hartford.

Page 8 – Rearing Ponds, Kettle Brook Hatchery. Photograph copied from the *Fifth Biennial Report of the State Commissioners of Fisheries and Game, 1903–1905*, Hartford: From the press of Hartford Printing Company, Elihu Geer & Sons, 1900, p. 966. These reports are in bound volumes at the Connecticut State Library, Hartford.

Page 10 – Loading a trout-stocking truck. Photograph taken by the author on August 29, 2011, at the Burlington Hatchery, Burlington, CT.

Page 12 – Bringing a trout to net. Photograph from the Photographic Collections of the Connecticut State Library, Hartford.

Page 18 – Comstock Bridge over the Salmon River. Photograph from the Photographic Collections of the Connecticut State Library, Hartford.

Page 24 – Landing a trout on the West Branch of the Farmington River. Photograph of Patrick Keane taken by the author in 2003, the year he began fly fishing.

Page 26 – Tatiana Lvov, fly fishing on the Farmington River. Dr. Lvov learned to fly fish as a young girl in her native Russia. Her husband, Yuri Lvov, snapped this photograph in 2010.

Page 27 – Patrick Keane shows off a nice catch. Photograph taken by the author in 2003.

Page 32 – A fly fisherman working the tail waters. Photograph from the Photographic Collections of the Connecticut State Library, Hartford.

Page 42 – Reggie Galvin and his 6'0" backpacking fly rod. Photograph of fly rod by the author. The Photograph of Reggie Galvin was supplied by Nick Flynn of Williamstown, Massachusetts.

Page 48 – West Cornwall Bridge over the Housatonic River. Photograph from the Photographic Collections of the Connecticut State Library, Hartford.

Page 59 – Fishing a quiet spot in hip boots. Photograph from the Photographic Collections of the Connecticut State Library, Hartford.

Page 67 – The "Old Stone Bridge" on the West Branch of the Farmington River. Photograph by the author.

Page 76 – Fishing in a nice pool below a Culvert. Photograph from the Photographic Collections of the Connecticut State Library, Hartford.

Garnet Books

About the Author

Kevin Murphy is an independent historian and writer who lives in Rocky Hill, Connecticut. He is the author of *Water for Hartford* and *Crowbar Governor*.